ERIC MORECAMBE: LOST AND FOUND

WEEK COMMENCING MONDAY, AUGUST 23, 1948

"LES FILLES DE CHASSE"

Produced and devised by Nat Tennens

1 **JIMMY BENNETT & SYLVIA BEBE**

Musical Entertainers

2 **MORCAMB & WISE**

Direct from the Windmill Theatre, Strike a New Note in Comedy

3 **ARTISTIC STUDIES by DESIREE, assisted by MARIE TONI, LILLIAN, JOAN and PHYLLIS**

4 **FRANK FORDE** .... Voice from Australia

5 **DAVIDE & DESIREE** .... The Exotic Dancers

6 **JOSE DEL RIO** .... Ropes and Wisecracks

In accordance with the requirements of the Lord Chamberlain—(1) The public may leave at gangways, passages, and staircases must be kept entirely free from chairs or any other obst ways intersecting the seating or to sit in any of the other gangways. If standing be permitte indicated in the notices exhibited in those positions. (4) The safety curtain must be lowe programme

Intermission : Kilburn Empire Orchestra

7 **THE NAITOS** .... Marvellous Foot Equilibrists

8 **TED LACEY & ROMA**
Two People—Comedy and a Piano

9 **AFTERNOON AND LATE NIGHT STUDIES**
Desiree and the Girls

10 **MORCAMB & WISE** .... More Laughs

11 **OLIVE DALE** .... In New Songs

12 **LEON PIERRE & GANG**
The Most Novel Act in Vaudeville

We acknowledge with grateful thanks the valuable help given us by Messrs. Arding & Hobbs for the sports equipment and floral decorations.

General Secretary ...... J. Welton   Manager .... A. E. King
Stage Manager .... F. Roberts

end of the performance by all exit doors, and such doors must at that time be open. (2) All
ns. (3) Persons shall not in any circumstances be permitted to stand or sit in any of the gang-
the gangways at the sides and rear of the seating, it shall be strictly limited to the number
nd raised in the presence of each audience. The Management reserve the right to alter this
eir discretion.

ERIC MORECAMBE: LOST AND FOUND

GARY MORECAMBE

The Robson Press

First published in Great Britain in 2012 by The Robson Press
(an imprint of Biteback Publishing Ltd)
Westminster Tower
3 Albert Embankment
London SE1 7SP

Frontispiece: from a 1948 variety bill. Notice that
Morecambe has been spelt incorrectly! – GM

ISBN 9781849543361

10 9 8 7 6 5 4 3 2 1

A CIP catalogue record for this book is available from the British Library.

Set in Sabon
Cover design by Namkwan Cho

Printed and bound in Great Britain by
CPI Group (UK), Croydon CR0 4YY

CONTENTS

FOREWORD
BY MIRANDA HART

••

If someone were to ask me what the most memorable day of my life was, I would, with relative ease, answer: 7 May 2011. This was the day that I was asked to visit Eric Morecambe's widow, Joan, and his son, Gary, at the house where Eric and Joan had lived since 1968. They had read that I had been inspired by Eric's work and was a fan and very kindly got in touch to see if I would like to meet them and come to the house. I jumped at the chance.

Now I confess I have never been married or had children, so I am not sure whether a wedding or the birth of a child would bump this day into third position of wonderful days in my life. I have a suspicion possibly not and it might remain firmly at number one. I'd better explain.

Put simply, Eric Morecambe is my hero and inspiration. From an early age, he has had a profound effect on my life. For those of you who have bought this book, you might feel similarly. You might be able to say, hand on heart, that Eric is your hero. He's your chosen dinner-party guest of all human beings past and present. He's your favourite comedian. Well I concur. But for me, and I hope I don't lose all of you here, it was more than that.

In Eric Morecambe, I felt I found a friend with whom to share my life. Such was the immediacy of his humour and the warmth of his on-screen persona that I would put on a Morecambe & Wise video on a gloomy day, a day when the Black Dog might have been prowling, and the show would gently wash over me, lifting my mood. He would help me escape from how I was feeling, relieve the darkness. It wasn't just in bad times. I would laugh at him as I was laughing about positive things in my life, thereby sharing joyful moments with my beloved comedian too. He was there for me. I am not sure there are many comedians who are that open, endearing and approachable in their work to have such an effect on audiences. He was, simply, unique.

So, how did it all begin, this passion and some-times obsession with Eric Morecambe? I was born on 14 December 1972 and I imagine that I would have been in my mother's arms, or upstairs with the noise of laughter creeping upwards, a couple of weeks old, as they watched that year's Morecambe & Wise Christmas special. I like to believe some sort of comedy osmosis began then, right at my very beginning. In my opinion, and I believe Gary Morecambe agrees with me, their best sketch and when they were at their absolute peak of brilliance was the 1971 Christmas special André Previn routine. It is incredible to think they had been working as a double act since 1941, their first television show *Running Wild* was broadcast in 1954 and there they were in 1971 at the height of their game. Not only were they popular enough to maintain audiences over so many years (and increasing audiences) but also they were always improving, always evolving, always working, so that after thirty years as a partnership and seventeen solid years of television they produced one of their finest comic moments.

It is well documented that Eric was concerned the sketch wouldn't work. Amongst other things, they were unable to rehearse the hours they normally would because of André's availability. But, luckily

3

A souvenir programme for Morecambe & Wise's 1964 summer season at the Wellington Pier Pavilion in Great Yarmouth.

A fan shares a joke with Eric at a Lord's Taverners
charity event.

for Britain, they didn't drop it and forty years later you can often hear one of its famous lines being retold. 'I'm playing all the right notes, but not necessarily in the right order.' At the end of the sketch, I believe you can see the relief, joy and excitement in Eric's face as he claps, realising that that was probably the best thing he had ever done. He was clearly aware of the pure magic that had just happened on stage – everything had come together to create something truly special. And his face in that moment proves how important it was to him, how much he wanted things to work so as to avoid letting himself or the audience down.

So, in 1972, our national treasures were riding high on the previous year's success and they produced another fine programme for the nation to savour at Christmas. It's strange to think I had only just been born when sketches such as miming along behind Jack Jones in pink dresses to 'Dream Dream Baby', the 'Life is a Cabaret' ending with Glenda Jackson, and the iconic image of Eric and Ernie dressed as reindeer were first being aired. They are part of my heritage now and so familiar to me forty years on. The BBC website still runs clips of that reindeer sketch. And what a testament to Morecambe & Wise, and all the creatives behind the show, that it can stand that test of time. There aren't many entertainers you can watch repeatedly and still find funny even when you know what's coming. As Jimmy Carr said to me once, there are some comedians who audiences just want to be in a room with, just want to watch, be in their company, it doesn't really matter what they are doing or saying. And there are some comedians for whom the script and their jokes are the selling point. Jimmy was putting himself in the latter – his razor-sharp one-liners, his close-to-the-knuckle shocking gags – these are things the audience is expecting from him as he maintains a formal, fixed position centre stage. Eric and Ernie as performers belonged to the former category. Of course the sketches were brilliantly written and honed, but it was Eric's character – energetic, playful, silly – that we were desperate to spend time with. He drew us in. He could say and do very little and we would laugh. So, even now, when we know what's coming, we have a childish excitement just to be in the room with him again. His work doesn't tire.

I was about five or six when I actually first remember watching a Morecambe & Wise show. I don't know exactly what sketch or programme it was. It would have been 1977–78, so it could have been their last BBC show, or the first one on Thames

Sheet music for the song 'Pretty Little Black-Eyed Susie', as performed by Eric and Ernie.

Television where they moved for their final years in 1978. All I remember is dancing along to a routine and being absolutely mesmerised when this round-faced, puffy-eyed, cheeky man smiled a ridiculous grin at me down the camera. I distinctly remember the feeling it gave me. Obviously, I laughed. But I also remember feeling loved, like a best friend was inviting me into their play world.

Since that day I have not only found a friend in Eric Morecambe, but I have also had a need for the 'silly'. I have wanted to play. I always hated being told 'don't be silly' when I was younger. It used to make me very cross indeed. And I can distinctly remember thinking, 'If Morecambe & Wise can be silly and have fun in life, when they are grown-ups, then I am going to darn well be silly too!' I think I probably knew then, in some way, that I wanted to be a comedian. And from that age, in terms of televisual watching, they had instilled the need for big, bright, light entertainment shows to pour gently over me and wash the trials of the day away. Other favourites of that generation that I would watch, according to my parents, standing mesmerised, mouth agape, quite close to the television, included Tommy Cooper, Joyce Grenfell and *The Two*

Ronnies. But it was Morecambe & Wise and Eric in particular who had my heart.

In my late teens, I realised for certain that I wanted to be silly for a living. I wanted to be in comedy. I wanted to give people what Morecambe & Wise gave me. I saw the effect of their job, as we would all sit down as a family and watch, tears of laughter pouring down our faces. I wanted to see whether I could be in what I thought was a very important industry in bringing those emotions to people in their sitting rooms. What a gift. It seemed like a very arrogant thing to want to do, so it took me twenty-six years to admit it.

In my early twenties, or rather 'the tricky post-university, trying to cope with the real world for the first time' years, the *Eric & Ernie Live* video got me through. I knew it backwards. I was particularly enamoured by a video of their live theatre show, as opposed to the TV recordings. It made their work even more immediate and exciting. And, for me, it's them at their funniest. They seemed more alive, more free, less guarded and formal in their delivery. I suppose the pressure was off. They had the thousand-strong audience in front of them, but it was contained to just that. Their television shows at this point were getting twenty million plus viewers.

That's serious pressure. But here that was momentarily relieved. They were completely natural, slightly cheekier, and slightly rougher round the edges, doing what they did best. And what, I suppose, they were born to do. I loved it. Still do. So *Eric & Ernie Live*, the video, was my refuge in my early twenties. I spent many a night, when my friends were all out clubbing, learning the dance routine they did to the song 'Pretty Baby'. I would learn a couple of the moves, pause the video, rewind to make sure I had it, and continue until I could do the whole routine with them. Not the most usual pastime for a young person just moved to the bright lights of London, but I was happy. Although, I confess, no one knew (probably until now) exactly what I was doing!

I had an extraordinary day two days before going to see Joan and Gary, when I had been asked by Ronnie Corbett (another comedy hero) to take part in a programme he was making for ITV about young comedians and who had inspired them. He asked me to choose an iconic place that related to a comedy hero, and we would go there to film for the day.

Without hesitation I said Fairfield Halls in Croydon where the *Eric & Ernie Live* show was recorded. I had never been there but I could visualise the stage, the curtains, the floor, the wings so clearly and I knew I would dearly love to see it for real. So, on the morning of 5 May 2011, I arrived at Fairfield Halls and Ronnie, on camera, showed me around. We arrived at the stage door and walked the walk that Eric would have done to the stage. I suddenly stopped in my tracks. Ronnie asked me what was wrong. I had seen the beginnings of the wood floor of that stage I knew so well from the video. My heart started racing. I was going to stand on the very place Eric stood all those years ago. We walked through the curtains and I was confronted with a surprise. They had put an old 1960s microphone, just like the one Eric and Ernie used, and a band at the back of the stage (again, just like the video) and, when I walked on, the band burst into an arresting version of 'Bring Me Sunshine'. I was transported. And then I cried. And then I did the Morecambe & Wise dance across the stage a couple of times! 5 May 2011 was probably the second best day of my life.

As I got older, temping in offices and trying to pursue my dream of getting into comedy, Morecambe & Wise's legacy kept me going. They reminded me

Taken from a 1970s souvenir programme which was sold at Morecambe & Wise's one-night concerts.

of the necessity of laughter in the world. It was hard work, very hard work to get into the industry. It took me seven or eight years to get my first job. But I will never forget when I walked into BBC Television Centre for the first time – I was totally overwhelmed by the fact that this is where Eric and Ernie worked. Eric would have trodden the same corridors as I now was. Along with Tommy Cooper, Tony Hancock, The Two Ronnies. Such a rich history. That feeling when I arrive at the BBC never leaves me. Now, when I am feeling like writing is too tough, I go and stand at a balcony that overlooks one of the studios they filmed in. There is a big picture of Morecambe & Wise in black tie leaning against a lamp post in the gallery. I look down and imagine them on the floor recording my favourite sketches. One of them being the silliest and simplest of routines involving Eric miming with horses' reins, sitting on a carriage. Ernie is singing a love song to his 'girlfriend', Eric is a Russian-looking carriage driver. Every half a minute or so, Eric says, 'Giddy up,' and is then pulled out of frame by the reins as the horses in effect suddenly speed up. His Russian hat goes flying, his fake moustache comes loose, he then climbs back up on the carriage and starts again. I know what's going to happen, but I still find it hilarious. And you can see Eric's joy in doing it too, his tiny wry smile colluding with the audience. 'We all know what's happening here,' he is saying. 'We don't know why it's so funny, it just is.' I look down and imagine him filming that. I remember what I owe him, and it keeps me going.

Each year that I work in comedy, it seems to get harder, more pressure, trickier to think of new ideas. And with that I become fully aware of the sheer hard work, the dedication and sacrifices Eric would have made for his long career. Recently, I started to become incredibly grateful to this man who probably pushed himself far too far, to the detriment of his health and sometimes possibly his family life. I know he worked on a Christmas special while on a family holiday in the summer and generally found it hard to switch off. But he did this predominantly to honour his audiences and make them laugh as much as he could and to the best of his abilities. Gary and Joan might have wanted their father and husband more present on a holiday, but I am one of millions of audience members grateful for the energy he gave to his job. I don't think there are many entertainers who are as committed as he was; who believe so wholeheartedly in what they are doing; who do their job for others not just themselves. He knew

The waxworks – lit for surreal silhouette effect.

M&W were approached to front many different projects during their 1970s heyday, but this must rate as one of the strangest – astrological sign reading! – GM

that people needed another Morecambe & Wise show and he wasn't going to let them down. And he pushed himself to the limit to do this over a forty-year career spanning radio through television at the BBC, then ATV, BBC again for the 'golden years', and finally back to ITV, ending in 1983.

So I am very grateful to Eric for being a friend through good times and bad, for making me laugh, for inspiring me to get into comedy, and all this by smiling that famous smile down the camera lens. From the moment that first happened I dreamt of having my own show on the BBC when I could look down the camera to people in their sitting rooms myself. I didn't think it was remotely possible I would ever get a show made, let alone one that some people might watch and like. And I find it exciting and humbling to think that, when I smile down the lens, I might be having a small per cent of the effect Eric Morecambe had on me. I have him to thank for it all.

So, with all that he meant to me, all those shows that I had watched, all those books I had read and pictures I had studied of him with his family in their family home, on 7 May 2011, I was suddenly heading to his very house to meet Joan and Gary Morecambe. I was incredibly nervous. Could I just quiz them all about him? Are they bored with talking about him? Would I get over-emotional? I drove up to Harpenden from London. I had my dog with me. I was about half an hour early, so I pulled up in to a field to walk the dog and pass the half hour. I took her off the lead and, in the one moment I took my eye off her, she found some fox poo (or possibly something worse) to roll herself in. Nightmare! I couldn't turn up to Eric Morecambe's house with a stinky, shitty dog. I had a water bottle with me and poured the water all over her to try to rinse it off. No dent was made in the overwhelming stench. I was convinced I could hear Eric's voice from on high laughing: 'Brilliant, wouldn't want it any other way.' It was a hot day, and I arrived in a bit of a nervous sweat explaining that my dog reeked so she would have to stay put in the car, and apologies if I smelt at all odd but I might have some fox poo on me. Not the best of starts.

But Gary and Joan were absolutely charming, kind and lovely. But what was surprisingly hard to deal with, however, was that as I walked into their sitting room I realised that everything was the same.

Eric with former Doctor Who *actor Tom Baker. This would have been taken at a charity event prior to their working together on Charles Wallace's* The Passionate Pilgrim.

I recognised the curtains from a photo I had studied of Eric in a book. I sat down on a sofa. Gary explained that was where Eric would sit to watch his own shows. It was the same sofa. The only thing that was different in the room was the television. There were photos everywhere. I found it incredibly moving. I couldn't believe I was so close to him. I felt a sort of grief. As if I had just found out about his death. He's so alive on the shows I re-watch. But here, despite a presence, there was a hole.

After a lovely lunch (amazingly with some of my favourite food, to add to the perfect nature of the day), Gary asked if I would like to see his father's study. Of course! We walked upstairs and into a calm, quiet room that overlooked the garden. Gary explained this was the room where his father would do all his writing and thinking. When he was here, he was not to be disturbed. As I took it in a bit more, I realised that this was just as it would have been too. The bookshelves had all his notepads in, old books, clocks, awards. Gary showed me the smoking jacket on the back of the door – with the elbows worn out from leaning on the desk. The coat I had seen in photos that he wore at Luton football ground was also hanging on the same hook. It was all still there. And then I nearly jumped as I saw a

21

little face peering out of a cardboard box. It was Charlie. Charlie the ventriloquist dummy from the live video I had watched over and over again. Gary let me pick Charlie up. I did a couple of the jokes that Eric did while holding it (most notably 'his mother was a Pole') and worked out how to move his eyes. Eric had touched this. It was so extraordinary. I had to bite my lip not to cry. I didn't think it was my place to cry. Gary might think me very odd weeping over his father, whom I never knew. A particularly difficult moment was when (and he had given me permission to snoop) I opened a box – it was a pipe box. The smell of tobacco hit you as if he could still be in the room. It was all a bit much. It was as difficult as grieving for a long-lost family member or very close personal friend.

I bumped into Stephen Merchant (another Eric fan) a few days before I was going to the house, and told him about my offer to visit. He was gobsmacked. I said I would ask Gary if he minded if he came along too. But Stephen said not to. He said he thought he'd find that a bit too much. A bit strange and possibly difficult. I thought that seemed odd. I thought he was mad for missing out. But, standing in that study, I got it. Eric was an entertainer who meant so much to his viewers, probably particularly to those of my and Stephen's age who started watching him in our formative years, that we did treat him like a father and brother.

After a cup of tea, I felt I might have outstayed my welcome – I could have stayed for hours more, days in fact. I felt really at home. But I pulled myself away. And, as I turned out of the drive, I found myself bursting into tears and I could not stop the whole drive home. I got a few strange stares at traffic lights as I blubbed uncontrollably. I kept saying to myself, 'This is ridiculous, why am I crying so much?' I reflected and realised the day was a culmination of my life. I remembered feeling the silliness and joy of being a child watching Eric. I was grieving for the tough times when I watched him for respite. I was finally patting myself on the back for getting into comedy and I felt overwhelmed with tiredness at how the job had taken its toll. But I realised it was worth it. I was in a job that sells love and joy, without which no one can flourish. And when I wasn't flourishing, there was Eric. And I was more grateful than ever for his dedication to providing such abounding love and joy. It was the best day of my life because it punctuated all that had come before it.

You might think I am being over the top. And I am sorry, and slightly embarrassed, if it sounds it.

A message
from your President,
Although a little hesitant
Is not without its precedent
Three years I have been resident
'Cultivate hilarity,
Keep working for the Charity'

God Bless.
Eric

But I am just telling you how I honestly feel. And I don't think I will be alone. I think the strength of our feelings shows the importance and particularly resonance of comedy. But most of all they indicate the unique creation and genius that was Eric Bartholomew. How extraordinary that an ordinary boy from Morecambe could have a life that affected so many people, so deeply. Thank you, Eric.

Thank you, Gary and Joan, for my 7 May 2011. Thank you for the honour in asking me to write this foreword. And thank you for continuing Eric's legacy by providing us with this new book.

Miranda Hart
London, 2012

ERIC MORECAMBE: LOST AND FOUND
AN INTRODUCTION

First and foremost, this book is a celebration of a British icon who also happened to be my dad!

I joined the Morecambe & Wise bandwagon in April 1956, but was not conscious of it until after my fifth birthday when I saw my father on TV for the first time, which is when he and Ernie started broadcasting their half-hour Morecambe & Wise shows for ATV. This coincided with my arrival at primary school, and, at this first rung on the educational ladder, I came into regular contact with the earliest TV critics – none of them older than eight! What they gave me was an understanding of how Morecambe & Wise were perceived outside the four walls of our

The author with his dad! A publicity shot we had taken in 1982, prior to a joint appearance on Russell Harty's chat show. – GM

28

house. It is not surprising therefore that this was the moment I chose to put my father on a pedestal.

Just because he was on a pedestal, and has remained there for me even now as I write these words at the tender age of fifty-six, doesn't mean every day is a rose-tinted memory. As a father and son, we could argue quite easily – but Dad and comedian Eric Morecambe were two different things to me, and they were to him, too, as he mostly referred to their double act in the third person.

I suppose that, until I was a teenager, squabbling or doing anything that was considered unbecoming was completely off the agenda. But what a ten-year-old might go along with, a seventeen-year-old does not.

It's strange to recall that even my teenage angst (what little there was of it) was diffused by his humour. It's really difficult to be the defiant child when the parent doesn't outwardly disagree with any opinions you have, but with comedic precision exposes the limitations of your thought processes. And it was so difficult to outrage a man who never understood the meaning of embarrassment.

The only way to upset my father was to mention Ernie Wise in a negative way. He could say what he wanted at any given moment about his partner, but that wasn't a licence for you to join in. It's something I've given much thought to in recent times, and my conclusion would be that each was very protective of the other – they'd been together since the age of twelve or thirteen. 'Closer than brothers', their scriptwriter Eddie Braben has described them. I wouldn't argue with that. I know, for instance, that they would finish each other's sentences in a manner suggestive of a childhood spent together.

I wrote in an earlier book about my father that it would certainly be my last written work about Eric Morecambe. And so it would have been had not circumstances contrived to occasion what you are now reading.

It began on a visit to my mother's house at the beginning of 2011. On arriving at the old family home, filled with childhood memories coloured by my father's massive personality, I found her in the kitchen waving a copy of *The Times* newspaper in her hand. She showed me a photo of my father taken at a Luton Town FC event. It was a photo neither of us had set eyes upon. 'Imagine how many photos of Dad must be out there that we haven't seen,' she remarked, unaware what impact those words were to have on me.

'Yes,' I nodded. 'Wouldn't it be great to collect some of them and put them into a book so we have a permanent record?'

It was just a throwaway comment, but one that would lead to precisely that end. At that particular time though, the thought of trawling through my own and others' personal photographic collections, as well as those of the media, to collate photos of my father was not a realistic one. I was busy with other things, particularly directing a run of short films for transmission on selected satellite TV channels, and my intention never to do any more Morecambe & Wise-related books had not been formed lightly. I'd been writing books related to my father on and off for some thirty years – surely that was enough!

A friend and erstwhile colleague Paul Burton was directing another short film I was producing at Elstree Studios. In a coffee break, I mentioned the photo my mother had seen. 'It would make a great book,' he said, and immediately offered his services for research purposes, it being one of his main lines of employment and one area that had been dulling my enthusiasm. Another step towards taking an idle thought and turning it into a reality was unexpectedly made.

Two more made it impossible for me to turn down the opportunity of making the book a reality. While discussing the idea with Paul Burton, I mentioned the vague notion of making the book to my longtime publishing friend of some thirty or more years, Jeremy Robson. Jeremy had published several of my previous titles, including *Behind the Sunshine: The Morecambe & Wise Story*, and *Cary Grant: In Name Only*, both of which I co-wrote with the author, playwright and *Coronation Street* script-writer Martin Sterling. Jeremy said it was a wonderful idea and just the sort of title to which they could do justice.

Finally, I mentioned the idea to my newest friend and Morecambe & Wise fan, comedienne Miranda Hart, taking the liberty of asking her if, should this book happen, she would be willing to write a foreword. 'Willing!' she told me. 'It would be an honour.'

And so the process of creating a book of rare photographs – certainly the vast majority of which I had never seen before – began and into the mix came some curious memorabilia from my father's former study, and memories of those who, however briefly, came into contact with him.

Rummaging through my father's mine of papers

and photographs always quickly puts me in mind of Morecambe & Wise. The TV shows come flooding back, the classic lines so easily remembered. 'Have you got the scrolls? No. I always walk like this!' 'I'm playing all the right notes, but not necessarily in the right order!' 'He's not going to sell much ice cream going at that speed!' 'What do you think of it so far? Rubbish!' And so on. You would think I would be bored of it all by now, but, if boredom for the subject hasn't struck me in my mid-fifties, then it is unlikely it ever will.

The nation's enduring love for the duo never fails both to amaze and inspire me. Last Christmas, they were on TV in a documentary, a *Parkinson* interview, TV specials and a film (spanning three different channels) eight times! The previous festive season gave us Victoria Wood's touching, if not wholly accurate, account of their first meeting and early days on the road through to their first break in television.

Their influence is still felt: Madame Tussauds in Blackpool last year put them into their wax figures exhibition. Two stage plays – David Pugh's

The widows (Joan Morecambe and Doreen Wise) with the wax figure copies of their iconic husbands.

and Kenneth Branagh's *The Play What I Wrote* and Bob Goulding's *Morecambe* – won major awards, and author William Cook's publications *Eric Morecambe Unseen* and *Morecambe & Wise Untold* were wonderfully produced works bolstering the Morecambe & Wise canon, which continues to build to this day. It's truly remarkable considering that Eric died nearly thirty years ago and Ernie over thirteen.

Out of everything in recent years, it is the made-for-TV film *Eric and Ernie* by Victoria Wood and scripted by Peter Bowker that touched me the most. It captured the era from which they emerged and, despite the liberties that film-writers have to take – and Peter Bowker is no different

– it managed to give a good insight into Eric and Ernie's upbringing. There was a warm portrait of Sadie, Eric's enduring and supportive mother and the force behind the beginnings of the double act.

Sadie is a book in herself. Often erroneously portrayed as a single-minded showbiz mum, pushy and determined to see her son achieve greatness on the stage at all costs, and bereft when Eric and Ernie finally outgrow the need for her support, her true input and interest in the act was far less definable. As is often the case, the reality is more prosaic than the idea our imaginations conjure of what she should have been like.

If Sadie was ever pushy or determined to see her son succeed, it was because she recognised the balance between her son's talent and his self-acknowledged idleness, and wanted him to take the opportunity that talent gave him to lead a better life than the one offered to him in 1930s northern England. She possessed surprisingly wide vision for someone of her station in life. And, as for supporting Eric on the road, she couldn't wait for someone to come along (firstly Ernie Wise and, later, my mother Joan) and take him off her hands. Husband George at home must have felt he'd been widowed! So, instead of a feeling of sorrow at her son's departure to new pastures, she embraced his going away with a huge sigh of relief and made a welcome and permanent return to Morecambe Bay and husband George. Her self-appointed mission to get her son off to a good start had been achieved. She never again involved herself with the workings of their act or their partnership.

Victoria's film, however much amended for televisual purposes, still gave me a lump in the throat when watching it. It certainly prompted me to re-examine the act's earlier years and lose myself if only mentally, while sitting on long flights or train journeys, in that time. My appetite had already been whetted prior to Victoria's film by a trip I'd made four years earlier to Morecambe. I was researching that 'last' book on my father I referred to, and happily that led me to the last people still alive who had not only known Eric as a child, but either had attended dance class with him or been his mate at school. I'm still overwhelmed when I look back to my interviews with these now elderly contemporaries of my father who were part of his own humble beginnings. And what struck me the most was an observation that each one made to me, separate to the others' knowledge – that they would have been more surprised if my father had *not* become the

My sister Gail with her paternal grandfather, George. – GM

superstar he became than the fact that he did. Considering the social background and challenging times in which his childhood was played out, that was quite a passing observation to throw out there. And it was delivered with such intense honesty by each of them that I couldn't help but recognise that it was no 'with hindsight' addition: they clearly had noticed that he was an unstoppable force, something we, his family, would come to understand, and which as a turn of phrase perfectly sums him up.

Perhaps it was that research period, as well as Victoria Wood's film, that encouraged me to wallow in my father's past – a past that was not mine, but which would form my own roots.

The idea that Eric and Ernie's story began before the Second World War never fails to stagger me. They are remembered as arguably the greatest double act Britain has ever seen – comedians whose shows brought in on average around twenty-five million viewers. Yet, when Eric and Ernie set out on their path to showbiz glory, Charlie Chaplin was still making silent films in a very youthful Hollywood,

Winston Churchill was yet to defeat Adolf Hitler and none of the iconic Beatles had been born. This gives a simple reminder of the sort of journey Eric and Ernie undertook, and the sheer graft involved in not only achieving what they did, but also the number of decades that their journey covered.

They were single acts working for Jack Hylton's youth shows when they first decided to team up. In fact, August 2011 marked the seventieth anniversary of that historic moment when, for what would be the first of many, many times, they stepped out together under the lights of the stage. Their debut came at the Empire theatre in Liverpool – billed as Bartholomew and Wiseman.

In a world of instant gratification, it's almost incomprehensible that they should have taken those first joint steps as fifteen-year-old youths and continued to do exactly the same thing (as massive stars) several decades later into late middle age. It must have taken tremendous dedication, particularly as their world had begun in the dying days of the variety halls when many of their friends and peers were sinking without trace as television increasingly slipped into people's living rooms, eventually annihilating most other forms of entertainment – particularly the variety show tours.

My father's profound observation on their ever-increasing success over the decades was that it happened because 'we stayed together'. There is a great deal of truth to be found in that. TV mogul and family friend Michael Grade correctly picks up on the fact that they made it a rule very early on that no bickering that might naturally occur – or something worse – would be allowed to enter their relationship and distract them from their goal of being a very good double act. That kept their relationship intact, both personally and professionally. They were also two of the most talented people operating in show business, with a remarkable enthusiasm to rehearse, develop and hone their skills. As people who knew them both in a working capacity often tell me, they would still be thinking of ideas for a show they had already recorded, even though any change or addition was beyond question.

One of the other reasons they had such longevity is very obvious – they loved being entertainers. As a young lad, I stood side of stage when they were doing the summer season in Great Yarmouth in the mid-1960s, and again when they were touring their own live show a decade later. Each time they were about to step out onto that stage was like it could have been for the very first time back in Liverpool, such was the hunger and enthusiasm for their work. The money and the glory were only by-products of what they were doing as an act. The act was everything. My father would have performed alone in the family kitchen if that was what it took. Come to think of it, he sometimes did! Indeed, living with my father was like entering a twilight world of Morecambe & Wise. When you recall that a fair part of each Morecambe & Wise show was built around a studio-created apartment with bedroom, kitchen and living room, there are strong echoes of our home life. Fortunately, we were spared the rituals of his act – the bits of business such as the wiggling of the glasses and the slaps around the face; even *he* would have been driven insane by that. But if you picture a moment the comic you knew as Eric Morecambe in a more silent repose – some of the energy and mischievousness lurking within, while simultaneously under a tighter control than you are familiar with – you would get someway towards seeing what it was like living with this comedy giant.

Morecambe & Wise's journey in show business

TOP: *Eric's daughter, Gail.* BOTTOM: *Gail and brother, Gary.*

through the decades wasn't solely about going from an unknown act to giant stars of television. There were many distractions on the way. The first being radio. Radio was around a long time before television forced it into a more ornamental pose in the household kitchen. For, as TV's presence increased, radio gave up its place in the living room, where families had gathered to listen to their Prime Minister delivering sombre reports on the economy or the war effort, or enjoy light entertainment such as *Workers' Playtime* and *Band Waggon*.

Eric and Ernie made their radio breakthrough on these shows and to my mind radio was the key to their developing such a powerful cross-talk act. They were working in theatre simultaneously, and travelling up to record the radio shows in Manchester on the Sunday between theatres, learning their scripts during those journeys. As it was radio and therefore (obviously) non-visual, all their skills were delivered solely through the voice. Not an easy thing for a double act, especially Morecambe & Wise's, which increasingly would come to depend on those little looks and asides. Think of all the times Eric would turn to camera and say, 'This boy's a fool.' Or the look he gives when André Previn calls his bluff with 'But you're playing all the wrong notes!' Not easy trying to picture such magical moments through sound alone.

I recently listened to some 1940s and 1950s radio recordings of Morecambe & Wise we still have stored on original vinyl. What struck me was how well they dealt with this new medium – the way that they chose to compensate for the restrictions radio put on their act was to speak louder and faster! (Interestingly, decades later Eric gave that very in- struction to their guest star Glenda Jackson during rehearsals for a BBC TV show.)

It shouldn't go unmentioned that another reason Morecambe & Wise became so strong as a come- dy force is the fact that they were allowed to. They were given something denied to most entertainers these days – time. We live in an era where instant results and success are obligatory to avoid being swept aside; nurturing is almost a forgotten notion, banished to the dead world of previous generations.

My father always said that he accepted he and Ernie had some talent, but even then – back in their heyday of the 1970s – he always balanced that by adding that they were so fortunate to have been in the right place at the right time to display their wares. They were a young double act beginning to blossom just as TV began to enforce its dominance over radio as the popular form of home entertainment.

It wouldn't happen now, of course, for Morecambe & Wise didn't succeed right away on TV – indeed, they were somewhat written off after failing to register in their first series outing in 1954, *Running Wild*. In our frenetic world of the new millennium, such a disaster would have meant no second chance. And their shows would be too expensive to make today.

Fortunately, during the 1950s and 1960s, they were allowed to fail on TV and then return a few years later in a new series, finally showing how well honed they had become as a partnership when given the freedom to perform in the way they wished to perform, not under the directives and orders of the TV station. That wasn't the final package. Morecambe & Wise continued to further refine their personas and relationship through the ATV years 1961–67, and into the BBC years 1968–77. Development into the Morecambe & Wise we know and love to this day was mostly due to their BBC scriptwriter Eddie Braben dispensing with the traditional variety-hall hardness of the typical straight man, Ernie Wise, and the dumbness of the typical comic, Eric Morecambe. Ernie became the mildly flamboyant know-it-all with pretensions to being a playwright – 'the play wot I wrote' – and Eric became more streetwise and divisive with trace elements of Phil Silvers and Groucho Marx, on the one hand comforting the guest star, while destroying their credibility on the other. Perhaps they relaxed more and more into these new roles as time passed, but fundamentally there were no noticeable changes from 1968 until the end of their working lives.

During that twenty-year reign as kings of comedy, Morecambe & Wise went to Pinewood Studios and made three films in the mid-1960s, *The Intelligence Men, That Riviera Touch* and *The Magnificent Two*. But they never found the big screen to their liking and vice versa. Their comedy was always intimate – perpetual middle-aged men (even when they were young they appeared to be middle-aged men) sometimes almost whispering to each other in cross-talk banter to an attentive audience in the studio and living rooms across the land. Not so on the big screen. There was no audience reaction to comfort them, and they tended to disappear in lots of stunts – long before CGI could provide a degree

· ·

TOP: *Eric with his favourite 'Sherlock Holmes' pipe. He had a matching deerstalker at one time, but sensibly hid it. He is also seen here with part of his watch collection, which grew into quite a serious passion and included rare wrist watches and fob watches.* – GM

BOTTOM: *My sister Gail with our mother, Joan.* – GM

of comfort. These 1960s films crop up on TV with surprising frequency, and I watch them with not a little nostalgia, remembering clearly my father going off to make them. And they're really not that bad. They just aren't that good, either.

My father was quite tense during this period. *The Morecambe & Wise Show* for Lew Grade's ATV was steaming along nicely, but I sensed that, while the films were an irresistible challenge to the duo, and they were clearly on a roll after years of endlessly treading boards and performing at the end of piers, they were also a thorn in the side. Firstly, they were clearly out of their comfort zone, and, secondly, they were doing something that took a reasonable amount of their time away from the television studios where they worked best.

My father was always ambivalent whenever I referred to those Rank films of the 1960s. 'Not really us' and 'they were all right, I suppose,' were the most positive reactions. Other times it was, 'They were rubbish really' or 'they tried to make us part of the Norman Wisdom vehicle'.

The only other film they made – and which in his final days my father managed to prevent from even being seen on TV for a number of years, let alone on a big screen anywhere – was *Night Train to*

Murder. Personally I found it murder to watch, and it is nothing in comparison to my father's own opinion. It really rankled with him. Opinion is split. Some people come up to me even today and describe it as a little-known gem. It's a subjective issue, but what let it down from my viewpoint were the poor direction and editing, and the extreme slightness of the script. There is nothing edgy about the story – indeed, it's quite turgid – and not enough gags punctuate what little storyline and action there is. Yes, it is a film in which they are supposed to play characters, but it was essentially a Morecambe & Wise film – that's where the emphasis is and why the film got made in the first place, and with the expectation that their names brought to such a project.

If you look at one of the Morecambe & Wise TV shows, such as the routine with John Thaw and Dennis Waterman, you'll see it's filled with sharp gags, quick asides and splendid movement. Of course, TV is very different from cinema. There is no ad libbing as such when shooting a film, and many other characters – too many – were crammed into this particular production. That had always been the secret of Eric and Ernie's appeal and the reason why they finally made it on TV. As soon as the cast of thousands disappeared, just leaving them and a guest

star or two, their brilliance was able to emerge. And now, at the final hour of their working life together, they had unwittingly allowed themselves to be cajoled into something clearly marked as average before filming had even begun. And that's what rankled with my father – his failure to have spotted that it wasn't anywhere near right for Morecambe & Wise. At the time he beat himself up badly about it, but with the benefit of hindsight we now realise that there were reasons it slipped past his normally flawless judgement: the man was ill and not going to live much longer than another month or two.

There are two distinct eras to Morecambe & Wise – their living legend and their posthumous one. It's rare in entertainment for deceased entertainers to receive the respect and glorification that accompanied them during their lifetimes. It could be argued that Morecambe & Wise are as successful today as at any time during their working lives. The TV shows and films continue to be repeated. The tributes, both verbal and practical, continue to pour in. 'Bring Me Sunshine' and their iconic skip-dance never go away and have appeared in adverts and greetings cards. Singer Robbie Williams even used it on one of his tours. He also had a very visible poster of Eric and Ernie on his stage set. Lee Mack uses a poster of them plastered to a door in one of his TV shows. Miranda Hart references my father constantly in her asides to the camera. Russell Brand, Jonathan Ross, Chris Evans have all referenced Morecambe & Wise within the last month of my writing this, so too the *Daily Mail*. *The Sun* used their image on the front page when announcing the coalition of Cameron and Clegg, plastering these politicians' heads on to Eric and Ernie's skip-dancing bodies. Though they are dead, their images and influence often reappear. As a double act, they are almost unique. Only *almost* because Laurel and Hardy are referenced the same way and, like Morecambe & Wise, live on in the public psyche.

The question I'm always asked in interviews, and which follows on to that observation just made, is: why do I think my father was and is so popular? I probably ask myself that question at least once a week (which shows how I fill my time these days). Both Morecambe & Wise had integrity, which is a key issue here. The pair went into the entertainment industry because they genuinely adored the working environment and were absorbed with the idea of entertaining the public. The public at large is not stupid – they can recognise a phony. More-cambe & Wise spent years entertaining that public with complete honesty, with no hidden agenda or smugness about them. And for the first two decades there was very little positive return. That they would go on to become a massive part of 1960s and 1970s TV entertainment was never guaranteed, but they stuck with what they knew and did their best. I believe the public appreciated this as they unwittingly became exceptionally familiar with these two characters that would never go away.

One of the clearest and earliest signs of their growing relevance as performers emerged when Eric nearly died at the young age of forty-two following a massive heart attack. The warmth of the public concern for his wellbeing was overwhelming. Their first comeback appearance was at the Pavilion Theatre, Bournemouth. They stepped out on stage with their usual enthusiasm to be greeted by a five-minute standing ovation. It prompted the thereafter oft-used expression by Eric to Ernie at the beginning of most shows – 'Do we have time for any more?'

Above all of this, and probably the most significant factor when attempting to analyse the longevity

Ronnie Barker

Dundee
5·4·83

My dear Eric –
I enclose a Haygarden card (sent originally to Miss A. Bangs, I notice) and also one of the cards you kindly sent me. Could you please sign it and send it back? I would appreciate it if you could also include a recent passport-size photo and any spare money you may have –
Yours, Ronnie

Two comic legends together. Ronnie Barker and Eric were good friends and great admirers of each other's work. They often communicated by postcard.

Ronnie Barker once recalled the time he and his wife had the Morecambes over to dinner. On arriving, Eric enquired who else would be coming. Ronnie happily informed him. Eric turned nonchalantly to his chauffeur, Mike, and said, 'Make it about an hour!' – GM

of Morecambe & Wise, is the indisputable fact that they were so wonderfully good at what they did. I still watch the André Previn sketch in awe. And, to give Previn his due, it is a three-man comedy success story. I'm glad to read that Miranda Hart, Jimmy Tarbuck and Victoria Wood go along with me in voting it their favourite piece of work by the duo. It was only one smallish part of the Morecambe & Wise 1971 Christmas show (which also included another memorable routine – putting the boot on Shirley Bassey), yet it ran almost the length of an episode of a sit-com. How wonderful that they were allowed to let it run its natural length without compulsory cuts and changes. In today's viewing climate, where we are considered to have the attention spans of goldfish, the Previn routine would have had to go out at about three minutes!

I think the final piece of the puzzle of Eric's personal longevity lies in his use of the camera. By turning away from Ernie and talking to the camera directly – stepping outside the performance and entering your and my living room – he was becoming a part of the viewers' household, another family member. Miranda Hart was quick to spot the intimacy of that device, probably when she was a young girl watching their shows back in the seventies, and it has certainly been very well incorporated into her own series *Miranda*. Yes, she has reinvented the wheel, but in doing so she has made it her own. Comedian Harry Hill uses the same device in his *TV Burp* series.

Another question I'm frequently asked, and which takes us into very different territory, is: what was it like to have Eric Morecambe as a father?

There is no straightforward answer. People can behave very differently from day to day, so I can only give a general overview in my response. Firstly, whenever I think of my father – and that's very frequently, probably every day – I at once picture him at the peak of his comedic powers (circa 1975) with a big grin on his face. That can't be a bad image to have of someone thirty years after they've gone. I know the cynics amongst you will question why I should have an image that's linked to his professional persona, but I honestly cannot recall much about his appearance in his final days when he was around the family home, as I had by then married and was living away. My mind's eye has no doubt chosen the more comforting option of him at his incredible comic best, the image we still are fed today on our television screens. As I've more than implied, my father lived and breathed show business, so, while I certainly do have warm images of him at home sitting in his office or by the swimming pool, they tend to be overshadowed by his own personal love of being a comedy star and this was when he was happiest. I would go so far as to say that that is how he would want to be remembered. You must bear in mind that this was a man who would sit down and watch his own TV shows and fall about laughing – that's how much it meant to him.

Growing up in the same house as Eric Morecambe was overall a very pleasurable experience. I'd worshipped him from the age of five. I very much doubt I perceived subconsciously that one day his career would play such a big part in my own life, but I know that once I knew what he meant beyond the family, and in doing so realised how unusual that made him, I never really stopped orbiting him. I watched his career go from strength to strength, and even for a short period indirectly worked for him when I was in press and publicity for his agent Billy Marsh at London Management. We both found the situation slightly comical come to think of it.

My father was a good, kind man with a fuse that had been shortened by the stress of his work and the expectations people invariably had of him. Perhaps his mistake was trying to live up to those expectations, but to be honest it was in his nature and upbringing to give his utmost and behave decently and properly, so he was never going to be one to knowingly let anybody down, or simply not care enough. Also, Morecambe & Wise were treading new ground – no one had really preceded them in moving successfully from stage to radio to TV. There was no blueprint on how to protect yourself from the bandwagon they'd climbed aboard as young kids. Consequently, I had a father at home who never could quite switch off or turn down anything work related. He could be very relaxed in certain situations – he loved watching TV, fishing, painting, reading, walking and bird watching – but the comedian in him was always lurking inside like a rogue spirit looking for that opportunity to burst out and perform with a quip or amusing observation. While much of that was in his nature, I did sense that some wasn't – that he was more grimly holding on in case he switched off altogether and could never switch back on again. Indeed, he actually said that to me.

Near the very end of his life, he was unable to make

....

Eric removing Ernie from his will! – GM

any major decision about his future – his health was clearly hindering his work. And yet, following meetings at the studios, he agreed to make more series of *The Morecambe & Wise Show* – surprising considering he had gone to those very meetings with the idea of announcing a partial if not total retirement. Presumably, all considered, he weighed up the fact that it had taken a long time for him and Ernie to get their big break, and that, having reached the stars, saying no to anything on offer was not a genuine option, even if it was a genuine thought.

The energy required for their shows, and required to become and then *be* Eric Morecambe – suppressed or otherwise – was quite exhausting to be around. And I'm sure it played a big part in his premature death, because, as comedian Rowan Atkinson observed, if it was tough to be around, imagine what it must have been like for him. As I've said before, and my mother has too, my father probably was, in a sense, a victim of comedy.

It's interesting to me to recall how intense my father's relationship with show business was. He wasn't particularly interested in the socialising, partying side of the business, purely the business of making comedy shows. For while I genuinely feel his desire to be funny waxed and waned in his last year or two of life – and it's no coincidence that his physical health was a frequently recurring issue by then – his desire to construct Morecambe & Wise shows never did. Hence, his inability to reject offers for more Christmas specials and a further series or two. Being funny was very tiring; creating and working on ideas with Ernie and their writers, working on which guest stars could be used in an appropriate manner and then, finally, recording the shows still ignited him – after forty-three years! Will any of our current crop of comedians have careers spanning over forty years? Not only is it doubtful but possibly unwise too. Having no precedent to speak of meant Eric and Ernie were making up the rules as they went along. Perhaps that is the difference these days – comedians form their own production companies and do things on their own terms: they know what is right and what is wrong for their physical and mental wellbeing, and have employed agents and secretaries to handle all the external elements of their business. Perhaps the extent to which today's comics run their affairs has gone a little too far in the other direction, removing them from their 'real' personality. Certainly, the likes of Morecambe & Wise would never have even considered it.

The last twenty-five years have seen a huge change

– the emergence of a self-preservation mentality, which overall should be considered a change for the better. My only mild discomfort with this more corporate approach to entertainment is when I sometimes watch a big-name stand-up doing his or her stuff at the Apollo Theatre or wherever, and find myself vaguely uncomfortable – and a tad disillusioned – that here is a millionaire production-company-owning entertainer pretending to be one of the general public. It grates with the reality of their situation and takes us back to that 'P' word – phony – that Eric and Ernie could never have been associated with.

With TV comedy now having a definite perceivable history, the new kids on the block have something to look on and use as a guideline. One of the clearest realisations, which comic actors such as Rowan Atkinson have proved, is that if the world finds you funny they will still find you funny should you decide to take time out and make infrequent returns. Indeed, making yourself scarce can have great positive benefits. People won't forget you – a common phobia of my father's if he took any length of time out, and he hardly ever did. In fact, his worry was twofold – worrying if the public would forget them, or if the public would be bored by the repetition of seeing them. Unnecessary self-imposed stress, we might say; yet that very stress is what created and gave us the Eric Morecambe we knew, loved and still love. It is a dilemma that can barely be solved by analysis.

I hope you enjoy the words and pictures in this book that celebrate a man who brought so much happiness to so many millions.

Gary Morecambe
Portugal, 2012

ERIC MORECAMBE'S NOTEBOOKS

AGE – MALE and FEMALE

1. *You're getting old when you don't care where your wife goes – as long as you don't have to go with her.*

2. *Careful grooming and good make-up will take ten years off a woman's true age. But you can't fool a long flight of stairs.*

3. *Hello beautiful, where have you been all my life?*
Well, for the first half I wasn't born!

4. *A little boy and his younger sister put on some of their parents' clothes and knocked on the neighbour's door – and said – we are Mr & Mrs Brown and we have come to see you!*
    Taking it in their stride, the neighbour said – come in Mrs & Mrs Brown – and do have a drink. After serving a couple of rounds of lemonade the lady said – care for another glass of lemonade? – No thank you – said the little girl – we have to go home now – my husband has just wet his pants.

AGE   MALE & FEMALE.

1. YOUR GETTING OLD WHEN YOU DON'T CARE WHERE YOUR WIFE GOES — AS LONG AS YOU DON'T HAVE TO GO WITH HER.

2. CAREFUL GROOMING AND A GOOD MAKE UP WILL TAKE 10 YEARS OF A WOMANS TRUE AGE — BUT YOU CANT FOOL A LONG FLIGHT OF STAIRS

3. HELLO, BEAUTIFUL, WHERE'S HAVE YOU BEEN ALL MY LIFE?
   WELL, FOR THE FIRST HALF I WASN'T BORN

4. A LITTLE BOY AND HIS YOUNGER SISTER PUT ON SOME OF THEIR PARENTS CLOTHES AND KNOCKED ON THE NEIGHBOURS DOOR — AND SAID — WE ARE MR & MRS BROWN AND WE HAVE COME TO SEE YOU! — TAKING IT IN THEIR STRIDE, THE NEIGHBOUR SAID — COME IN MR & MRS BROWN — AND DO HAVE A DRINK — AFTER SERVING A COUPLE OF ROUNDS OF LEMONADE THE LADY SAID — CARE FOR ANOTHER GLASS OF LEMONADE — NO THANK YOU — SAID THE LITTLE GIRL — WE HAVE TO GO HOME NOW — MY HUSBAND HAS JUST WET HIS PANTS —

65

There's only one difference between him and a coconut – you can get a drink from a coconut.

That's a nice suit ... Didn't they have your size?

He said he would examine me for £5 ... I said if he found it, I'd split it with him.

I won't say how old she was ... but she was Adam's babysitter.

What a figure. 6 miles of bad road.

One day we were playing leapfrog. But I kept jumping too low.

When she drinks soup ... couples get up to dance.

He said the spotlight was helping his rheumatism.

You've been like a son to me ... Insolent, surly and unappreciative.

Times have changed ... You call a car dealer for a demonstration and he sends over three pickets.

I gave up women and drink ... and it was the most boring twenty minutes of my life.

THERE'S ONLY ONE DIFFERENCE BETWEEN
HIM AND A COCONUT — YOU CAN GET
A DRINK FROM A COCONUT

THAT'S A NICE SUIT .... DIDN'T THEY HAVE
YOUR SIZE?

HE SAID HE WOULD EXAMINE ME FOR
£5... I SAID IF HE FOUND IT, I'D SPLIT
IT WITH HIM   Xmas

I WONT SAY HOW OLD SHE WAS .. BUT SHE
WAS (......) BABY SITTER. Xmas

WHAT A FIGURE - 6 MILES OF BAD ROAD Xmas

ONE DAY WE WERE PLAYING LEAP FROG.
BUT I KEPT JUMPING TOO LOW

WHEN SHE DRINKS SOUP .. COUPLES GET UP
TO DANCE   Xmas

HE SAID THE SPOTLIGHT WAS HELPING
HIS RHEUMATISM -

YOU'VE BEEN LIKE A SON TO ME .. INSOLENT
SULLEY AND UNAPPRECIATIVE   Xmas

TIMES HAVE CHANGED ... YOU CALL A CAR
DEALER FOR A DEMONSTRATION AND NOT
SCADS OVER THREE PICKETS

I GAVE UP WOMEN & DRINK ... AND IT WAS THE
MOST BORING 20 MINS OF MY LIFE

• •

If her lips are like fire and she shivers in your arms ... give her up ... she probably has malaria.

Nudist camp. Where men and women go to air their little differences.

Two brothers – one went into politics and the other went straight.

He's a very smart dog ... I say, 'Are you coming or aren't you?' ... He either comes or he doesn't.

Then I entered coll. 4 years passed ... I didn't.

I didn't know whether to put up my hands and fight like a man or put my ears up and run like a rabbit.

Someone once told me I have three million organisms living on me ... And that's not including my brother-in-law.

He has no children ... He has a very strict mother-in-law.

It's better to be hot and bothered than satisfied and worried.

He who laughs last supports Chelsea.

At the sound of the beep you will hear the correct time ... You have just heard the correct time.

SAY DEAD

IF HER LIPS ARE LIKE FIRE AND SHE SHIVERS
IN YOUR ARMS ... GIVE HER UP ... SHE
PROBABLY HAS MALARIA.

NUDIST CAMP. WHERE MEN AND WOMEN GO
TO AIR THERE LITTLE DIFFERENCES

TWO BROTHERS — ONE WENT INTO
POLITICS AND THE OTHER WENT STRAIGHT.

HE'S A VERY SMART DOG ... I SAY ARE
YOU COMING OR AREN'T YOU ! ... HE
IETHER COMES OR HE DOESN'T.

THEN I ENTERED COLL. 4 YEARS PASSED ...
I DIDN'T .

I DIDN'T KNOW WHETHER TO PUT UP MY
HANDS AND FIGHT LIKE A MAN OR PUT
MY EARS UP AND RUN LIKE A RABBIT.
Xmas

SOME ONE ONCE TOLD ME I HAVE 3,000,000
ORGANISMS LIVING ON ME ... AND THATS NOT
INCLUDING MY BROTHER IN LAW

HE HAS NO CHILDREN ... HE HAS A VERY
STRICT MOTHER IN LAW

ITS BETTER TO BE NOT AND BOTHERED
THAN SATISFIED AND WORRIED Xmas

HE WHO LAUGHS LAST SUPPORTS CHELSEA Xmas
(SUCH GASTER)

AT THE SOUND OF THROBLE YOU WILL HEAR THE CORRECT
TIME — YOU HAVE JUST HEARD THE CORRECT TIME
Xmas

. . . .

A characteristic page from Eric's notebook.

GAGS

MAN. HAVE YOU GOT ANYTHING FOR AN UPSET
STOMACH.

CHIC. YES

MAN WHAT

CHIC HIM (POINTS TO ERN). HE UPSETS MINE.

ERN WHEN I WAS A BOY ——

CHIC WHEN YOU WERE A BOY THE FASTEST
THING IN THE WORLD WAS A HORSE !

FILM. PERSON MALE OR FEMALE IN HOTEL
FOYER READING MAG. UP TO HER
FACE. IT LOOKS AS IF THE PICTURE ~OF~ ON
THE MAG. IS THE LOWER HALF OF THE
PERSON LOOKING OVER MAG.

TELEGRAM ON PHONE. TELEGRAMS? IS LAST GT.
LONDON W 4 — WEST 4 FOUR YES. MOTHER
ILL FATHERS BROKEN HIS LEG SISTER PREGNANT
GETS MARRIED NEXT WEEK STOP. ECT. ECT.
PARDON? — (TO ERN) DO YOU WANT IT SENT
GREETINGS ? !

D
E
F
G
H
I
J
K
L
M
Mc
N
O
P
Q
R
S
T
U
V
W
X
Y

71

WITH
AT ESTATE AGENTS. IN HOUSE BEING SHOWN ROUND
HOUSE. IT HOSNT GOT ANYTHING WRONG WITH
IT HAS IT? YOU KNOW LIKE DRY ROT OR ANY
THING — GOOD LORD NO SIR ITS AS GOOD
AS B.HAM PALACE. (TAPS DOOR IT FALLS DOWN)
HAVE YOU HEARD FROM PRINCE PHILIP THEN

ERIC. THERE'S A MAN OUTSIDE WITH A KNOCKOUT
COAT.
ERN GREAT COAT.   X
ERIC. THAT WHAT I SAID. ITS A GREAT — COAT.
                          —
GIVE HIM A GET WELL CARD AND SEND
HIM HOME.

JUST BEEN TO LOCAL CINEMA TO SEE THE SLIMY SEXY
ONE EYED MONSTER — THE MANAGER BEEN THERE
FOR YEARS.

INSURANCE — 2d A WEEK 50 YEARS. 90 YEARS
I KNOW ITS NOT MUCH. BUT ITS A START
IN LIFE.

DO ME A FAVOUR, HIS EARS WERE SO BIG
YOU COULD DRINK OUT OF ONE OF THEM.
HE LOOKS LIKE A TAXI WITH THE DOORS
OPEN. I KNOW THEY DON'T CALL HIM

···

Many of the lines on this page – 'He looks like a taxi with the doors open', 'Give him a get well card and send him home' – became stock gags for Eric to be called upon on numerous occasions. Until now, I never realised they were anything other than spontaneous, but, as with the best of his lines, they were written down and no doubt mulled over for quite some time. – GM

ERIC MORECAMBE:
IN HIS OWN WORDS

....

This is perhaps my favourite insight into my father's own early years that he ever consigned to paper. What I really enjoy about his reminiscing is it clearly comes from a genuine sense of nostalgia for that time and place, and as such is void of Eric Morecambe the performer. Other than his brief excursion into keeping a diary, I can't recall any other time he wrote purely from the heart and without a gag every other line.

No one ever believes this, but my mother would have always verified it for me. My earliest recollection is of when I was nine months old. I remember being put on the kitchen table at our

home in Buxton Street, to be wrapped in a coat and long scarf before being taken out in my pushchair. I can also remember that the roof of that house had caved in, and that was why we were the first on the list to be moved to Christie Avenue by the council.

I only know as far back as my great-grandfather on my dad's side, who brought his family to Lancashire from what was then Westmorland, but is now Cumbria. So we have been Lancastrians for approximately a hundred and fifty years or so. By coincidence, my grandparents on my mother's side were also from Westmorland, but came down some years afterwards.

I remember making an inkwell at school during woodwork lessons – we didn't call them carpentry lessons in those days, you know. I could have been no older than seven or eight. This inkwell that I proudly presented to my parents was in fact just a plain lump of wood with a hole skewered in the middle. You couldn't have put any ink in it. It was terrible! But my mother thought it was brilliant. 'Oh lovely, Eric,' she said when I gave it to her. Then she called my dad. 'Look, George. Come and see what our Eric has made.' She actually kept it, along with many similar items, throughout her lifetime.

I remember once going along with the family on a picnic to Hest Bank (on the edge of Morecambe Bay). I was ten at the time but I really remember it as though it was this morning. I would have to wear a blazer suit if I was going to look my best. That was short blue flannel trousers and a blue flannel jacket. We were standing at the bus stop waiting to go home when a thunderstorm started and it poured with rain. The whole of my suit seemed to become sponge-like, soaking up the rain as it fell. I began wiping the rain from my face and hands and legs with my jacket sleeves, but it wasn't just rain – it was blue dye pouring out from my suit. By the time I got home I was blue from head to foot.

I often have a chuckle when I recollect some of my father's endeavours. There was a time when I was a boy when I would sit and watch him catch starlings. He used a dustbin lid and a stick with a piece of string connected to it. Then he would put a lump of bread under the lid and use the stick to support it. When the starling went to have a nibble, he would pull the string and trap the poor little thing. He would catch between ten and twenty of these birds, kill them then give them to my auntie Maggie to bake in a pie. She needed about twenty, because when you pluck a starling you're not looking at too much flesh. I once had an airgun as a lad and he borrowed it to shoot a seagull off our neighbour's roof. He hit it cleanly enough, but it toppled straight down their chimney pot and into the fireplace round which the family was gathered at the time. That must have given them some shock.

I can recall walking with my mother by the river that weaves its way through Hest Bank. I was fifteen, and she turned to me and said, 'Now one day you'll be a big star, as long as you don't get big-headed. But when you are a big star, you'll buy me a house in Hest Bank, won't you?'

I nodded dumbly and said, 'Yes, Mam; I'll buy you a big house out here.'

Many years later, in the latter part of the sixties, whenever I saw her she would say, 'Well, you are a big star, and now where's my house you promised me at Hest Bank?' And eventually I bought her a home in Hest Bank.

MY LORDS.... SORRY. CHIEF BARKER, MY LORDS...... SORRY ABOUT THAT RONNIE....
~~CHIEF~~ RONNIE BARKER, MY LORDS, LADIES AND GENTLEMEN, FELLOW BARKERS.......

WHAT A PLEASURE IT IS FOR ME TO STAND UP.....AND TALK ABOUT A MAN WHO IS
SO MUCH LOVED BY HIS FELLOW ARTIESTES....... AND ONE OR TWO MEMBERS OF THE
V.A.F........ A MAN WHO IS KNOWN THROUGHOUT THIS COUNTRY AS THE CARY GRANT OF
RADIO ....

YES, IT IS A GREAT HONOUR FOR ME TO BE ABLE TO SAY A FEW WORDS ABOUT........
WHATS HIS NAME ...... AS I LOOK ALONG THIS TABLE, AT WHAT I CAN ONLY DESCRIBE
AS A MIDDLE AGED SPREAD. I SEE IN THE PLACE OF HONOUR, UNDER A CHALET LOANED
FOR THE OCCASION BY ~~ANYLETH~~...... I SEE ARTHUR ASKEY SAT OR STOOD THERE
.... WITH HIM ITS THE SAME EITHER WAY.

I SAY TO MYSELF, ERNIE.....OH YES, EVEN I GET MIXED UP... I SAY TO MYSELF, ERIC
THERE IS A MAN WHO HAS BEEN ENTERTAINING US FOR THE PAST 50 YEARS..... WHETHER
WE WANTED HIM TO OR NOT. A MAN WHO HAS BEEN A STAR SINCE 1939 WHICH IS ALMOST
20 TO 8.....A MAN..... I'M SURE HE WON'T MIND ME SAYING THIS, AND IF HE DOES
SOD HIM........A MAN OLD ENOUGH TO BE ERNIES FATHER..... AND LOOKING AT THEIR
SIZES, VERY PROBABLY IS....

HIS CAREER SPANS 50 YEARS.......SO HE WOULD HAVE KNOWN DES O'CONNER AS A YOUNG
MAN.   YOU REMEMBER DES.......DES......SHORT FOR DESPERATE....

I REMEMBER ARTHUR WHEN HE FIRST WORKED FOR V.A.T.......I MEAN A.T.V.   HE WENT
TO SEE SIR LEW GRADE......OF COURSE HE WASN'T SIR LEW THEN.... HE WAS JUST PLAIN
ORDINARY YOUR ROYAL HIGHNESS........ HE WENT TO SEE LEW AND ARTHUR WAS WEARING A
BROWN SUIT, AND LEW PICKED HIM UP, PUT HIM IN HIS MOUTH AND LIT HIM.....

TO STAY IN SHOW BUSINESS AS LONG AS ARTHUR HAS, YOU NEED THREE THINGS..... AND
IF YOU HAVE THREE THINGS YOU SHOULD BE IN A CIRCUS......

I AM ONE OF THE MANY PEOPLE WHO HAVE WORKED WITH ARTHUR......I'VE SHARED A
DRESSING ROOM WITH ARTHUR......I'VE SEEN HIM STRIPPED.....AND I MUST BE HONEST
I HAVEN'T SEEN MUSCLES LIKE HIS, SINCE CILLA BLACK STOPPED WEARING SHORT SLEEVES.

A MAN WHO IS KIND TO OTHER COMICS....GENEROUS TO HIS FRIENDS....I ONCE ASKED HIM
FOR A LOAN, AND RIGHT AWAY HE SAID 'CERTAINLY'.......HOW MUCH 10, 20, 50, A POUND.
HE'S LIKE THAT.......

Eric's short tribute speech for comedian Arthur Askey. I like the Ronnie Barker line. Eric and Ronnie were good friends.
— GM

Eric with one of his all-time comic heroes, Arthur Askey (centre of photo). I always felt my father was in awe of Arthur, and it probably had much to do with the fact that, when Eric first met up with Ernie as thirteen-year-olds, Ernie was already a child star courtesy of appearing with Arthur Askey at the London Palladium. I have no doubts that Eric would have been very impressed by this, and looked upon Ernie's mentor as very much his own, bearing in mind the closeness between Eric and Ernie.

Behind Arthur is comedian Dickie Henderson, who was particularly big on TV and stage in the 1960s. Dickie would later do the eulogy at Eric's funeral in May 1984.

Surrounding the three men are the singers The Beverley Sisters. – GM

GAIL MORECAMBE

Dad was very humble and very grounded. Ernie was always the ambitious one. I think Dad would probably have been happy to stay second on the bill.

My brother and I were brought up not to show off. I could never bring myself to say that my father was Eric Morecambe.

Summer holidays as a child were absolute bliss. I can remember staying as a family wherever Dad and Ernie were appearing in summer season. I had a horse and so we used to find the nearest stables where I spent all day indulging a fledgling equestrian passion. One year we took one horse and came home with a different one!

I would go to the theatre in the daytime with Dad to pick up the post. I used to sit out front at the

Eric at his most contented – an avid twitcher, he even took to taking books on European birdlife with him on family holidays abroad. While we trundled down to the beach for the day, he would wander off high and low with his binoculars and notebook. – GM

theatre and watch the show during the matinees, and I would get an overriding sense of joy from the audience and the special power Dad had over them. I recall that whenever Dad and Ernie went off stage the audience's shoulders would slump. They would be waiting for the other acts to finish and Dad and Ernie to come back on stage.

It feels like Dad has never really left. A day doesn't go by without there being some sort of a reference to Morecambe & Wise. I think Dad would be stunned that people still have the interest in them that they do.

I can remember Dad saying to me: 'Gail, when I'm gone, you will watch the videos? You will watch them? If you don't watch them, then it was all for nothing.'

I didn't have a problem seeing the shows in the period immediately after Dad died. Then, after a few years, watching them suddenly became much more painful, because when the end credits came on and the show finished I felt that sense of grief all over again. Fortunately, this didn't last long.

One Saturday, the family went to a wedding in Harpenden. In the morning, Dad had come through the kitchen door and looked at me. I had a feeling something was wrong; he didn't look well. With Dad, there seemed to be an everyday self and then someone who had a sixth sense about everything. Dad and I used to communicate on both levels.

Dad sat next to me in church on the Saturday and held my hand all the way through the service. But he had also taken care to clear out his drawers and put his affairs in order. He died on the Monday. The following week, I was sat in the same pew in the church for his funeral, looking at his coffin.

I remember that Mike Fountain, Dad's chauffeur, had called at around four in the morning to tell me that Dad had collapsed after the show in Tewkesbury; later on, the call came to say that he had died. I know his heart couldn't cope any more, but I was still shocked.

I now give talks to groups about Dad. I love doing them and it doesn't cause me too much stress; it fits in beautifully with my life and the profits go to charity. I speak for about an hour and show a few family photos.

As far back as 1971, Dad was saying: 'We [Morecambe & Wise] might get another year.' He never took success for granted.

I was immensely proud of him: a unique man and a dear father.

Eric with daughter Gail on a beach during summer season, possibly Blackpool. This would have been taken about a year before I emerged on the scene, so circa 1955. – GM

SIMON PEGG

I remember watching *The Morecambe & Wise Show* with my grandmother, back when Eric would pretend to leave the studio in his cap and coat.

But my earliest memory of Eric is of the Cossack sketch with the horse and cart. As Ernie serenaded the female guest star, Eric as the driver was repeatedly pulled off the carriage by the unseen horse. It got funnier every time he did it. I was breathless.

Back then, TV seemed like a magical world – and Eric was a huge part of it.

In some respects, Eric was one of the first alternative comedians, like Tommy Cooper. He played with the absurd and deconstructed convention. He gave the private joke mass appeal. I don't know a contemporary comedian who isn't influenced by Eric Morecambe.

Eric was basically silly but with immense intelligence. It's impossible not to find him funny, he exuded comedy.

Last Christmas, I watched Morecambe & Wise's 1972 Christmas special. It was so entertaining and outshines most contemporary comedy programmes.

I toured with Steve Coogan in 1998 and I remember we performed on the same stage of a theatre that Eric and Ernie once performed at. It was a good feeling.

I met Ernie at the BAFTAs and I said to him how much Morecambe & Wise had inspired me. It probably didn't mean much to him, but I loved having the opportunity to tell him; they are legends.

I used to think it was amazing that Eric smoked a pipe. I remember seeing him on a repeat edition of the chat show *Parkinson* and saying: 'Oh, he really does smoke a pipe; it's not just a comedy prop!'

Eric's appearance on *Parkinson* confirmed that he was just as funny in real life. I remember he told a story about how he had a heart attack so hilariously. It's extremely poignant to see it now.

Of all the programmes I remember made by Thames Television I remember *The Morecambe & Wise Show* the most.

Eric had funny bones. He was funny to his very soul.

Signing cricket bats with Edward Heath.

EDDIE IZZARD

It's difficult to say when I first became aware of Morecambe & Wise. I used to love to watch their series and Christmas specials with my dad and my brother. This was when I wasn't at boarding school. I wasn't able to watch the shows when I was there as no one was allowed to watch telly. My tastes in comedy later became more alternative but I loved Eric's naturalness and ability to ad lib. I liked his style and would have loved to be able to be funny like he was.

If you're classically good looking when you're at school, then you're instantly popular and social success comes very easily. The rest of the 95 per cent of us have to make up for this in some other way like by being good at sport, being cool, being bad or, as in my case, being as funny as you can be. I guess the latter is probably what Eric did in order to become popular.

Eric was like a kid playing in an adult's body; playfully pricking Ernie's pomposity in their various brilliant Eddie Braben sketches.

If Tommy Cooper and Eric Morecambe were alive today, I think they would be termed alternative comedians. Both performers played with the medium of comedy and broke the standard rules in their own unique way.

In the 'Grieg Piano Concerto' sketch, Eric did what no other performer had done or I think could ever do to a guest and that was to pick André Previn up by the lapels of his jacket with such excellent mock violence and take him down a peg with fantastically silly logic – 'I am playing all the right notes ... but not necessarily in the right order.' It's a brilliant sketch, highbrow and lowbrow at the same time and for me is the perfect example of a piece that sums up Morecambe & Wise. Eric's timing, and also impressively that of André Previn, is excellent.

The reason we will still be watching Morecambe & Wise in years to come is that their comedy is based in character play and is therefore timeless – as human character has never changed since the beginning of civilisation and I don't think it ever will.

Morecambe & Wise would have been funny even back in Greek or Roman times.

May 18, 1956

28

match of the Roses is on. The rest of the year we speak, though."

Morecambe told me how, wherever they are in summer season shows, they form a cricket team.

"We play all the local teams—lose every game, but there is plenty of fun. We had Harry Secombe playing for us one year, and d'you know, he's a very good bowler."

"We played a prank on Harry once," said Wise. "He was coming in to bat, walked all the way out to the pitch, took guard, looked round the field, took his stance, then we all walked off the field and left him standing there."

They soon took pity on him, and the game was resumed.

Morecambe and Wise are known to most people as "The Boys."

Said the charming Mrs. Wise : "They'll always be ' the boys,' even when they're 90."

But Morecambe says : "After this TV series I don't think we'll be able to live to 90."

They don't think TV is easy, then ? "We used to make cracks about TV," said Wise. "But not any more. We did a BBC series two or three years ago, and without thinking we called ourselves ' The boys who have nothing to lose.'

"Nothing to lose ? They showed us. We nearly lost everything. You should have seen the newspaper head-lines. Instead of saying ' Have you seen Morecambe and Wise ?' " (his voice swelled with elation, acclaim), people said " ' Have you seen Morecambe and Wise ? ' " (and his voice lowered to incredulous disgust).

Morecambe joined in : "We don't talk much about that TV series. We get an appendicitis pain if we do.

"Seriously, though, it was our fault the BBC series failed. This time we think we were more ready for it.

"We want to alter our style eventually to more situational comedy."

Wise nodded. "Anyway, that BBC series put us on the map. People got to know our name." He shuddered.

It was time for Morecambe and Wise to go on stage. We stood in the wings of the music-hall, waiting for a team of acrobats to complete their routine.

Had Morecambe and Wise never wanted to be acrobats ? Morecambe limped a few steps and said "Yes, once,"

Thus they fooled around, showing no signs of the nervousness both declared they feel whenever they are " on."

The band struck up their signature tune.

Wise inquired : "You can see all right from the wings, can't you ? Of course, it's not the same as seeing the act from out front."

Morecambe said cynically : "No, it's better back here."

And they were on.

Ambrose Willett

TWO suits a year are ripped to shreds by a young man named Ernie Wise—not his own suits. His partner's.

Ernie is "the belligerent half" of Morecambe and Wise, perhaps the brightest hope of Britain's more intelligent comedy teams and currently appearing in ITV's Saturday night *Winifred Atwell Show.*

Says Mr. Wise : "I get so excited. In the act I grab him by the lapels and the shoulders, and I must grab him too hard. The next thing I know the suit's ripped—they always go at the seams." He pointed to a tattered " bird's-eye " hanging on the dressing-room door.

But it's easy to buy another suit out of the considerable profits. Morecambe and Wise have been booked " solid " for five years.

They are aged 29 and 30, and have been a team since 1940, when they met as Bryan Michie " discoveries."

Morecambe—"I'm the melancholy one with the glasses "—agrees that he and Wise are equal partners, then adds : " It works out 75 and 25 per cent, of course."

Wise said nothing.

Homely name

Morecambe, whose Christian name is Eric, called himself after his home town.

" We've played Morecambe only once. Mum and Dad came along. Came twice, as a matter of fact." His voice sinks. " Couldn't believe it the first time."

How, then, did Wise get his name ? Morecambe " explained " :

" Well, Ernie's real name is Wiseman, you see. And there isn't a town named Wiseman, so we shortened it to Wise."

But, surely, neither is there a town called Wise ?

A momentary silence. Then Morecambe murmured : " We hadn't thought of that, had we, Ernie ? "

Wise disposes of the subject : " Well, Eric's real name is Bartholomew, so we couldn't call ourselves Bartholomew and Wiseman. It would go right round the bill."

They told me they worked out their act in the early days of the war.

SAID WISE : " We thought it was very funny. It was a yell."

SAID MORECAMBE : " We still think so. We've got used to it now."

Which reminded me : Didn't they sometimes forget that they'd been to a theatre before and do the same act again ?

" Always," said Morecambe.

" Look, we like to think we're progressive. So the other week when we hit a Glasgow theatre for the third time in 18 months we thought we'd change the act.

" We gave it a real chance. Monday, Tuesday, Wednesday, we did the new act and each night it died horribly. So Thursday we go back to the old act, and what happens ? It goes like a bomb—they cheer like mad. It's always the same if we try to change the act much."

They cheered up again on the subject of ambitions. Morecambe claims he and his partner have the same aim in life— " To own a bank."

Both are cricket fans. Morecambe (of course) is from Lancashire, Wise from Yorkshire—" so we don't speak while the

MORECAMBE'S IN LANCS, *BUT WHERE'S WISE?*

VICTORIA WOOD

··

I think we all have an image in our collective memory of Morecambe & Wise as two middle-aged men, with their backs to us, skipping. And probably lots of us can quote from the Mr Previn sketch with André Previn, and many of us may be unable to dissociate the music of 'The Stripper' from Ernie having a go at some grapefruits.

By they didn't emerge fully fledged as Britain's best-loved double act; they travelled a long road to arrive at that position. And it was that journey that interested me, particularly their early days in variety.

Eric and Ernie met as teenagers – Ernie the polished child star, and Eric the rather more reluctant embryo comedian.

I had thought for years that it was a story that

needed to be told and I am so delighted that we were able to bring it to the screen.

There is such a fondness for Morecambe & Wise, but I wanted us to tell a story that would mean something even more to an audience who had never heard of them. And Peter Bowker wrote a lovely heart-warming script that focused on their friendship, that bond that enabled them to weather the flop of their first television series, *Running Wild*, in 1954.

I was one of millions who loved Morecambe & Wise, and our drama (*Eric and Ernie*) was a way of celebrating their talent, their history and their endearing friendship.

Iconic skip-dancing poses by Eric and Ernie's scarily realistic waxworks. These were designed in 2011 for the permanent Madame Tussaud's exhibition in Blackpool, Lancashire.

BEN MILLER

....

You never really grasp what's going on with Morecambe & Wise until you see a picture of them in their teens. They are barely recognisable. Eric, in particular, looks nothing like his later middle-aged, iconic comic self – in fact, he looks more like a character from *The Beano* than a real person. They seem impossibly naive and fresh-faced. They have yet to become our beloved Eric and Ernie.

And then it hits you: this was serious. They threw their lot in with one another long before there was any way they could have known what they would become. They are so young, their act must have been founded on something more compelling than the odd well-told gag in some junior revue show. They must have been friends first and comedians second.

Comedian and family friend Stan Stennett (checked jacket) with Eric and Ernie and another performer in panto during the early fifties. Stan gave Eric and Ernie their first major break into the big time of showbiz when including them in the bills of his various annual productions. Stan is still ticking on nicely AND working, and I'm looking forward to having lunch with him in Bristol during late 2012. – GM

104

Nice to see Roger Moore peering over Eric's shoulder. Roger is a family friend, and became a regular guest star of David Pugh's and Kenneth Branagh's *The Play What I Wrote* (2002), a stage tribute to Morecambe & Wise. Roger told me that one of his deepest regrets was having been unavailable to appear on any of Eric and Ernie's Christmas shows, because it always clashed with his work commitments on the James Bond films. – GM

Eric and Ernie rehearse one of their famous flat sketches for an edition of their Thames TV shows.

Tommy Cooper, Eric and Ernie suddenly find they have company.
In the bar at Thames with TV producers/directors and 'talent'.
L-TO-R Robert Reed, Tommy Cooper, Dennis Kirkland, Eric, Philip
Jones, Ernie, Max Bygraves, David Clark, Malcolm Morris, John
Ammonds and Peter Frazer-Jones. – GM

One of the last, if not the last, TV interviews that Eric gave was
on an edition of *Good Morning Britain*, which aired on the ITV
breakfast station, TV-am. This footage has since been lost; however,
amazingly, this time-coded still has survived. – GM

Iconic skip-dancing poses by Eric and Ernie's scarily realistic waxworks. These were designed in 2011 for the permanent Madame Tussaud's exhibition in Blackpool, Lancashire.

LEFT The opening scene from their somewhat disappointing final outing together, their film *Night Train to Murder*. RIGHT Eric puffs on his pipe reflectively during a break from filming. He saw it shortly before his untimely death and remarked, 'It was not what we set out to make.' – GM

Eric and Ernie doing one of their in-front-of-tabs routines, this time with Hannah Gordon. – GM

Eric and Ernie separated by Thames TV Head of Light Entertainment, Philip Jones, long-time friend and great admirer of Eric and Ernie. He was part of the attraction for Eric and Ernie finally to depart the BBC and take their shows to Thames TV in 1978. – GM

Eric and Ernie take a break from taping a musical number for one of their Thames TV shows.

Eric and Ernie pose with the actress Gemma Craven on set.

Eric and Ernie (and Charlie, the dummy) doing their vent routine in an episode of *The Sweeney*, starring John Thaw and Dennis Waterman. Prior to this, Thaw and Waterman had appeared very successfully in a Morecambe & Wise Christmas show. A return invitation duly arrived – one presumes so *The Sweeney* could get their revenge on the double act.
– GM

ABOVE Taken during a break from filming the only modern-day scene in *Night Train to Murder*.

LEFT The double act of Mike and Bernie Winters was considered Eric and Ernie's competition. Contrary to popular belief, the four men were firm friends. As a child I recall summer seasons where Morecambe & Wise appeared down the road from Mike and Bernie Winters. My father would take me along with him in the afternoon so he could go and have a chat with them. One of Eric's best, if cruellest, jokes was when a BBC radio interviewer asked him what he and Ernie would have been if not comedians, and Eric answered, 'Mike and Bernie Winters!' – GM

Eric with the presenter Mavis Nicholson.

The adorable Suzanne Danielle obviously had an effect on Eric and his cigarette holder during a routine for an edition of one of Morecambe & Wise's Thames TV shows back in 1981. – GM

Rare photos of Eric and Ernie on the set of Denis Norden's Thames TV nostalgia show, *Looks Familiar*.

And that is what is at the heart of the appeal of any double act, from Abbott & Costello to French & Saunders to Mitchell & Webb. We want to know they get on. We want them to holiday together, preferably with their spouses and children in tow. We want them to be best men at one another's weddings. In Eric and Ernie's case, we even wanted to believe that they shared a bed.

Nowadays, far too many double acts end in divorce, or affairs, or stand-up comedy. But just because so many fail to go the distance, it doesn't mean that the great British institution of the comedy double act isn't still worth striving for. Morecambe & Wise were proof that it's possible. But, then again, neither of them had to put up with Alexander Armstrong.

KEN DODD

....

Shows ran from May to November and twice-nightly in those days and I had a plum spot in the second half of *Let's Have Fun*.

I used to watch Morecambe & Wise from the wings each night for the first few months of the long run and watched the duo perform their quick-fire humour. This was a time when comedy was becoming far more sophisticated and was leaving the red-nosed comedians behind. I believe this was helped along by performers like Danny Kaye and Bob Monkhouse.

Eric was like a playful imp. He had the perfect foil in Ernie. The foil or the 'feed' is the man who builds the structure of the act – and Morecambe & Wise

CENTRAL PIER

6.10 TWICE NIGHTLY 8.30 ★ BLACKPOOL

MATINEE - THURSDAY at 2.30

PRICES: 5/- and 4/- reserved

Manager: JOHN CAPSTACK Phone: 20423

SPECIAL SUNDAY CONCERTS

THE ORCHID ROOM
PRESENTS

'LET'S HAVE FUN'

WITH

★ MORECAMBE ★ AND  WISE

FROM 'VARIETY FANFARE'

★ THE KORDITES

TV. AND RADIO STARS

THE LAD OF LAUGHTER

KEN DODD

RITA SHEARER and her HAMMOND ORGAN

JOY HARRIS

HARALD NORWAY

JIMMY CLITHEROE

JIMMY HAMPSON

BERT MYERS

THE ORCHID ROOM "LOVELIES"

★ KENNY BAKER ★

RECORDING STAR

VOTED BRITAIN'S No. 1 TRUMPETER

108

were an excellent double act. I liked what they did and they liked my act.

Comedians have to build their own base when they're on stage. Double acts are different as they build a situation. A solo comedian can't do that as they have to feed off the audience. The audience is their straight man.

SIR BRUCE FORSYTH

I knew Morecambe & Wise from back when we were all struggling comics and were often on the same bill together.

I used to stand and watch them perform from in the wings. I knew even then that they had something special about them.

When we all first started performing in *Every Night at the London Palladium* together, I was top of the bill. One of their TV series was shown during the run and I could tell by the applause whenever they came on that they were becoming more popular because they were getting the same type of ovations I also used to get. At last they were finally receiving the success they deserved.

I also appeared as a main guest on a TV show

with Morecambe & Wise and the script had originally been written for Sammy Davis Jnr. to be the guest. Later, I also appeared with them in the tag of a sketch playing Santa Claus.

At one time, my musical director Don Hunt was working in the daytime as a musical associate on a series Morecambe & Wise were making. In the evening, he was working as the musical director on the show I was performing in. We used to pretend to have a fight during the show and I would shout things down to him in the pit and he would shout things back. As time went on, Don was starting to come out with funnier lines. In the end I asked him who was writing the funny lines for him. Was it the boys in the band? In the end he said that he'd told Eric about this part of the show, and so he'd started to give him stuff to say. It was a practical trick, and that was typical Eric – and he knew I would work it out!

It was so sad when Eric died. I was in Australia or New Zealand when I heard the news. I liked him so much as a person. You could have a serious conversation with Eric, but as soon as a third person arrived then he would turn into Eric the comic!

Morecambe & Wise's style will always be funny and will never date. Their performances and lines always made their sketches even funnier.

Bruce Forsyth proving that he not only regularly topped the London Palladium bill, but was comfortably above More-cambe & Wise! Bruce and Eric & Ernie shared the same agent, Billy Marsh. I worked for Billy in 1975, and I turned up to the office in a new suit and carrying a shiny new attaché case. I was suddenly aware that Bruce Forsyth had got into the lift with me. This was the very first time we met, and he had no idea who I was, of course. He took one look at me and my attaché case, winced a bit and said, 'What are you doing – selling brushes?' – GM

BRIAN CONLEY

I grew up watching Morecambe & Wise and recall that they were the first to encourage celebrity guests to appear on their shows. Although this isn't something new in these celebrity-obsessed days, it was novel back then.

Christmas stopped for *The Morecambe & Wise Show*. Their timing was spot on. They were consummate professionals and I was hugely influenced as a performer by Eric Morecambe. He was the thinking man's Tommy Cooper.

I used to love the put-downs Eric used to give each guest and the friendly banter they shared on their shows.

I admired just how much preparation Eric and Ernie used to put into all their TV shows. I think it's a shame that there's only really one video recording of their live act.

I loved the slapping dance, seen in their stage show, and this was one of my all-time favourite Morecambe & Wise routines.

The visual comedy influences Morecambe & Wise gave me and my act (from watching their shows) includes a joke with a false arm which they had used in a TV sketch. I borrowed this and used it in one of my own appearances later!

If I'd appeared on one of Morecambe & Wise's shows, I believe that Eric would have got my name wrong and called me something like Billy Connolly or Brian Connolly instead of Brian Conley!

I greatly enjoyed performing as myself in several performances of *The Play What I Wrote*.

....

OPPOSITE *The theatrical programme for* The Play What I Wrote. *This was David Pugh (Producer) and Kenneth Branagh's (Director) tribute to Morecambe & Wise. It was written mostly by (and starred) The Right Size – Sean Foley and Hamish McColl. All supporting parts were played by the multi-talented Toby Jones. Additional material came from M&W scriptwriter Eddie Braben, and me!*

It began proper in 2002, and transferred to Broadway in February 2003. It went on to be franchised using different actors and directors. I was consultant to the project – whatever that term actually means – and count those days as being amongst the happiest of my working life. It's not often you get the chance to have a bacon sarnie and a pint with Sir Kenneth! – GM

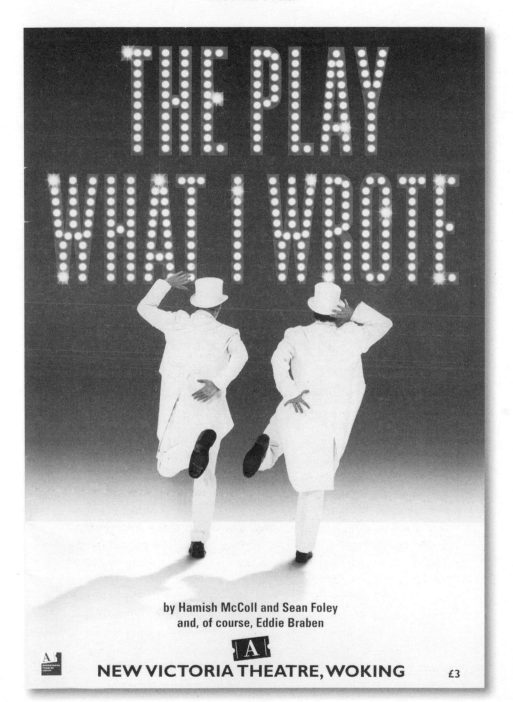

by Hamish McColl and Sean Foley
and, of course, Eddie Braben

NEW VICTORIA THEATRE, WOKING

£3

JIM DAVIDSON

The first time I met Eric was when I was appearing in panto during Christmas 1976 at the Alexandra Theatre in Birmingham. We did a midnight show and, although it wasn't a particularly dirty version, it did send the panto up. Eric appeared in the show and I remember that at one point he stuck his glasses in front of the curtains and brought the house down!

We move on a year or two to when I was appearing at the Wellington Pier Theatre in Great Yarmouth. I was walking to my hotel and saw Eric sitting nearby. I said, 'Hello, Eric!' and though he said hello he then blanked me, which I thought was strange.

Then a year later I was making *The Jim Davidson Show* in Studio 2 at Thames TV and Morecambe

Above: Willie Rushton, Pauline Collins, John Alderton and Eric pose for a photo at a Lord's Taverners charity event. Below: Willie Rushton with Eric at the same charity event.

Eric shares a joke with Judi Dench (her Damehood then still in the future) at a Lord's Taverners charity event.

121

& Wise were in Studio 1 rehearsing a *Jungle Book* sketch for one of their Christmas shows. At the pre-record, I was in their studio watching them and Eric saw me standing behind one of the cameras and stopped the rehearsal. I was worried that he was going to throw me out or something. But he walked over to me, shook my hand and told me he was pleased to see me and apologised for when we last met. He said it was only after I had gone that he remembered who I was. I thought this was so nice of him and it made me feel ten foot tall!

I worked at Thames with producer/director Johnny Ammonds, who had also worked on shows with Eric and Ernie at both the BBC and Thames. John wanted me to be more like Eric and Ernie and learn the script, and couldn't see why I wanted to do my own ad libs. Eric and Ernie always learned their ad libs and were meticulous when they were rehearsing.

I was very young and Eric was at the top, but he was very nice to me. He always had a glint in his eye. He liked comedians and I always wondered whether he had ever wanted to be a stand-up comedian himself and perform solo.

LIONEL BLAIR

When Joyce (my late sister) and I were appearing in *Kiss Me Kate* in Nottingham, Eric and Ernie were touring in variety and were also appearing in the city. The theatres faced each other and so we used to have coffee together. Eric was lovely to us, but Joyce and I were always rowing at the time and he used to tell us off!

When I did my first *Royal Variety Performance* in 1961, performing with Sammy Davis Jnr., Eric sent me a telegram jokingly saying: 'I hear you're the only one getting paid!'

When Eric and Ernie were appearing together in Blackpool, Eric used to come and watch us rehearse in the daytime for the TV show *Blackpool Night Out*.

Eric and Ernie often used to mention my name in their shows, like the sketch with Rudolf Nureyev. They were lovely. I wish I could say that I choreographed 'The Stripper' routine!

I was doing a PA in Cardiff, judging a competition. I got up early and saw on the news that Eric had died and I just burst into tears. He was only fifty-eight – he had so much more to give.

I loved him. He was a genius, brilliant, wonderful. I miss him.

At a Lord's Taverners charity event.

JIMMY TARBUCK

Eric Morecambe was as funny off stage as on, and was one off the block – an all-time great.

Eric was always generous. He took me aside one day and said: 'Young man, you have something. No one can tell you what it is, but never ask: "Why me?".' In other words, be yourself and don't try and analyse what makes you funny; if you do, you can make a terrible hash of your life.

To me, comedians come in two categories: men who say funny things, like Bob Monkhouse, and men who are funny like Tommy Cooper. Eric was the only man I have seen who could do both. When Morecambe & Wise were at their peak, with Eddie Braben writing the scripts, they were magnificent. Eric had the genius for taking good material and turning it into something out of this world, and in Ernie Wise he had the perfect foil.

Eric and Ernie always looked smart on stage, unlike some comedians today. Everyone wanted to work with them. And it was a great accolade if you got mentioned on their show.

Like a lot of people, my favourite sketch on *The Morecambe & Wise Show* was the *Grieg Piano Concerto* with André Previn. André was brilliant, especially as legend has it that he had very little time to learn his part.

I remember my first *Royal Variety Performance* in 1964. I shared a dressing-room with Eric and Ernie, Tommy Cooper and Denis Spicer the ventriloquist. While Eric and Ernie were rehearsing, Tommy Cooper unplugged the phone and locked it in a cupboard. I was still very much a boy in those days, and may have looked a little bit surprised. Tommy gave his confidential cough, and explained: 'You've got to watch these pros,' he said. 'While I'm on stage, they'll be phoning Hong Kong.'

Then it was Tommy's turn to rehearse, and Eric and Ernie came back to the dressing-room. Eric was on it in no time. 'Now then, Sunshine,' he said to me. 'Where's the phone?' 'Tommy locked it in the cupboard. He said you'd be phoning Hong Kong.'

Many royal charity events pursued Eric during the 1970s, and most he was happy to involve himself with. He was a great royalist, always deeply proud of his OBE.

Give Eric a grand staircase and a princess and he was in his element. Mind you, that's my mother closing in from behind! – GM

We had a laugh about it; then a few hours later we were all in the dressing-room waiting for the Queen to arrive. Suddenly, just down the corridor, the stage-door telephone started ringing. Eric had the answer. 'Tommy,' he said. 'It's long-distance in the cupboard!' Well, I just couldn't stop laughing!

That evening I was in the second half of the show. The others had been on, but I will never forget that Eric came down especially to wish me luck before I went out on the stage. It was typical of the man that he wanted to encourage a young fellow-comedian, and I have since tried to do the same for young comedians.

I recall that the Russian dancer Rudolf Nureyev appeared on *Sunday Night at the London Palladium* one week. Rudolf had a very, very big box, if you know what I mean! The next week Morecambe & Wise appeared and Ernie, in actual fact referring to Nureyev's appearance the previous week, said to Eric: 'Did you see it last week?' And Eric, quick as a flash, replied: 'I think we all saw IT last week!'

The *Bring Me Sunshine* show, staged as a tribute to Eric who had passed away in 1984, was a huge, huge night with a cast better than any *Royal Variety Performance* and how pleased I was to be part of it.

GEMMA CRAVEN

··

I was asked to do Morecambe & Wise's first show for Thames Television. That was the one that I appeared in as a French maid.

Later, for one of the musical numbers I agreed to do for Eric and Ernie, I had to jump into a tank of water. I am terrified of water! Despite this, I jumped in; it was only four feet deep – but I had to go under the water! I was terrified. I didn't tell them until afterwards. Eric loved that and gave me a big hug and burst out laughing. They then told me that no one else would agree to do it!

For the Christmas 1983 special we did a Mack and Mabel Keystone Cops sequence with Eric and Ernie both dressed as policemen. I was at the top of this ladder. One minute I could see both Eric and

Eric deep in thought as he and Ernie prepared to tape a sketch for one of their Thames TV shows, and then the pair in action.

Ernie below. The next I could only see Ernie. Eric had collapsed and the paramedics came and took him to hospital.

When Eric got better he came back and, bless him, finished the show. I greatly admired him for that. He came back and carried on as if nothing had happened. I remember him saying: 'Anything to give you lot a tea break!'

I am also so proud that I got to do the skip-dance with both Morecambe & Wise at the end of one of their shows.

They broke the mould when they made him. He was a one-off. A consummate professional and I loved him so much.

DAVID BENSON

The only time I met Eric Morecambe he gave me something very precious: a joke.

No doubt he gave almost everyone he met their very own private Morecambe joke. From what I know of him, he had a compulsion, an almost psychotic urge to make quips, to hear laughter. But what made this joke unusual was that he never even heard my laughter.

I should say that the first time I had seen Eric Morecambe in the flesh was in 1976, when I was fourteen, at the Alexandra Theatre, Birmingham. I am rather proud of the fact that the first time I ever went to the theatre by myself it was to see Eric and Ernie doing one of their live appearances in the 1970s. We got Ray Alan and Lord Charles, music

In the 1960s and 1970s, Eric was called upon to be at many charity events, this from 1969.

from an ageing, silver-haired male pianist, a juggler of some sort and The Beverley Sisters.

The second half of the show belonged to Eric and Ernie. In the mid-1970s, Morecambe & Wise were of course at the top-most peak of their career. The show they performed that night contained material they must have performed thousands of times over the years and yet, magically, it all seemed fresh-minted, almost improvised. Eric in particular had the great gift for making everything he said seem like a spontaneous quip off the top of his head.

I shall never forget him flapping his hands in his trouser pockets with that far-away, 'I'm not all there' look in his eyes, Ernie just watching him, the audience howling with laughter. It was a moment when time stood still: it could have gone on for ten seconds or ten minutes, that simple bit of business. Even now I cannot tell you *why* it was so funny. You just had to be there, I suppose.

In 2011, I played the Alexandra Theatre in Birmingham, and went and sat in the actual seat (more or less) where I sat back in 1976 and relived it all in my mind. I feel so lucky to have seen them perform at their best.

A few years later, I saw an advert in the *Birmingham Evening Mail* which informed the readers that

Eric Morecambe would be signing copies of his first novel at Hudson's bookshop. I skipped A-level history that afternoon and headed into town. It was only when I got to the shop that I realised I was in trouble: the book cost £7.99 and I only had five pounds on me!

Moving to the Humour shelves, I found an alternative selection, a mass-market book of jokes and pictures called *The Morecambe & Wise Scrapbook*, price £1.75. Perfect.

I joined the long queue of fans, all clutching copies of Eric's new book, some even pretending to read it. A sour-faced sales assistant made her way up and down the line asking, 'Have you got a copy of the book? Very good. Excuse me; do you have a copy of the book?' 'No, madam.' 'I'm sorry, he won't sign bus tickets. You must have a copy of the book. Do *you* have a copy of the book, young man?' she asked me. I pointed to my carrier bag. 'Yes, I've got the book,' I said, not strictly speaking the truth. It was 'the book' just not the correct book.

Let's just say, it had all the right words but not necessarily in the right order!

Somewhere at the head of the line I heard laughter so I knew he must have arrived. After a long wait, with my heart thumping wildly, the queue rounded

a bookshelf and there, just a few feet away, sat at a table was the real, actual Eric Morecambe, bald head, glasses, the lot. I noticed that he thanked every person whose book he signed, with an almost plaintive 'Thank you very much for coming!' as if they were old friends who had been to visit him in hospital.

When it was finally my turn, I cleared my throat and made the short speech that I had been rehearsing in my head for the last fifteen minutes. 'Mr Morecambe, I'm very sorry but I can't afford your book...' Everyone laughed, including Eric Morecambe – but not the bookshop employee. If looks could kill!

'Would you mind signing this for me instead?' I pulled the cheap paperback out of my bag. 'Not at all, I'd be delighted,' he said. 'What's your name?' He signed it and handed it back to me. 'Thank you very much. Thank you for coming,' he said.

When I got out onto the pavement I opened the book. He'd written: 'To David – Save up! Eric Morecambe'.

TED CHILDS

ric and Ernie had invited John Thaw and Dennis Waterman onto their Christmas show at the time when *The Sweeney* was very popular (1977–78). They afterwards said that they would like to take part in a *Sweeney* episode. We thought initially that it was a joke. However, when we realised they were serious, we had to decide what kind of episode we should contrive for Eric and Ernie's participation. We decided that, whatever we did, they should play themselves. Accordingly, the late Donald Churchill and I set out to write a script. We had to struggle somewhat to avoid the script falling between two stools, i.e. being neither comedy nor action drama. I must confess I have not seen the film for many years now but I like to think we pulled it off. Of

Cricket doesn't get better, or more politically incorrect, than this. But then this was the 1970s when clearly everything was acceptable. Eric is accompanied at this gratuitous shedding-of-clothes ceremony by former World of Sport presenter Dickie Davies. – GM

course, Eric and Ernie made their own very special contribution to the script which was what we really all wanted.

My recollection of shooting the film is that it was a hoot. *The Sweeney* in those days was geared to be a very cost-effective production and staying on schedule was a vital ingredient of our *modus operandi*. Although Eric and Ernie were very professional and fitted in with the 'kick, bollock and scramble' which characterised our production methods, their natural comedy and frequent ad libs brought us all to near hysteria on occasion with the whole cast and crew corpsed with fits of uncontrollable laughter and there were times when, as the man responsible, I wondered if we would ever complete the schedule. We did of course. Eric and Ernie were aided and abetted by John and Dennis, both of whom were closet comics.

BURT KWOUK

If you were asked to appear in *The Morecambe & Wise Show*, you didn't ask about the money – you just said: 'Yes!'

I recall being hired to do the 1983 edition of *Morecambe & Wise's Christmas Show*, but Eric became ill and so the cast were told that the show had been cancelled. Then Eric got better and we were all called to see if we were free to take part.

As Eric was well again, I had no inkling back then that this was to be the last TV show that Morecambe & Wise would make together.

At the time I was at the height of my fame playing the character of Cato in the *Pink Panther* films with Peter Sellers, so I imagine I ended up performing some martial arts movements in one or more of the sketches on the show.

My favourite sketches on *The Morecambe & Wise Show* have always been the most famous ones that featured the likes of André Previn, Angela Rippon, Glenda Jackson and Shirley Bassey.

Who made who laugh? Lord's Taverners President Prince Charles sharing a joke. – GM

MICHAEL GRADE

I had seen Morecambe & Wise work as a member of an audience, but in 1966 I joined Billy Marsh's agency as an apprentice and we shared an office and so I got to meet The Boys. I got on well with them and they liked me. I would sit in on their meetings with Billy, and chat and laugh with them.

It was a pleasure to see them work. I used to go to Borehamwood to see them recording their TV shows for ATV, and see them in concerts, pantomimes and summer seasons.

Eric and Ernie were immaculate in their dealings and very thoughtful. Once they made a decision, they kept to it. They didn't go home and change their minds.

If he had a crowd, Eric couldn't disappoint. He

liked the banter. He was exceptionally generous and would laugh at other comedian's jokes.

Because Ernie used to have Doreen (his wife) with him, I would go out with Eric and keep him company when they were away on tour. We got on very well. Eric and I shared a passion for football and went to football matches together. I can recall attending football matches with both Harry Worth and Jimmy Tarbuck.

My favourite recollection is of going with Billy Marsh to see Eric and Ernie in a summer season my uncle (Bernard Delfont) produced at the ABC Theatre in Great Yarmouth. They were trying out their famous ventriloquist stage routine for the first time. It ran to about four or five minutes. It was an absolute triumph and Eric was ad libbing away and Ernie was on fire. They were on cloud nine afterwards. By the end of the season the routine lasted about fifteen minutes.

It's important for me to say that I miss both Eric and Ernie.

MAVIS NICHOLSON

first interviewed Morecambe & Wise in 1970, which was the first year I appeared on television. During the first of two interviews that I did with them both, they ran rings round me and I couldn't get a word in – I couldn't stop laughing! The second interview I did with them was far more revealing. I used a trick of reading out their stars but didn't tell them which was theirs. For example: 'you are mean with money'; Ernie said, 'That is me.' At the same time as Eric said that is him. I was then also lucky enough to interview Eric alone after his first novel was published.

I appeared in Eric's first novel under the character name of Mavis Knickers. Eric sent me a chapter first to ask if this would be okay and said that he would

149

150

remove the name from the book if I wasn't happy. I was happy and honoured.

I believe Eric didn't want to be revealed as anything other than a wise-cracking fellow, even when he was off stage. He was like an uncle at Christmas who teased you. Maybe he was a shy person who used humour as a defence mechanism.

We love someone who can make you laugh to the point where tears are coming down your face. I laughed all the time when I was with Eric Morecambe. And I always felt he enjoyed watching you laugh. He beamed at you when you laughed at something he'd said.

On reflection, I can't pick a favourite Morecambe & Wise sketch, but I always liked the routines they did in front of the tabs the best.

TONY HATCH

I wrote the song 'Positive Thinking' specifically for Morecambe & Wise. (My former wife, Jackie Trent, co-wrote the lyrics.) The year was 1971. Eric and Ernie asked for something bright and cheerful that could work as an alternative TV-show closer to their usual 'Bring Me Sunshine'. They also included 'Positive Thinking' in their stage shows.

I knew Eric and Ernie quite well. Jackie had appeared on their TV show and was sometimes the female singing guest in their stage shows. I also met them frequently at Variety Club charity events.

'Positive Thinking' was my idea for the title. There had been a bestselling book in 1952 called *The Power of Positive Thinking* written by the so-called father of 'positive thinking', Norman Vincent

Peale. Even in the 1970s the phrase 'positive think-ing' was still in regular use.

I did a quick demo and Eric and Ernie liked it im-mediately. A songwriter can't ask for more. Their huge viewing figures made the song instantly pop-ular and they adopted it as their own. They also 'adapted' it because, in fact, the melody they sing isn't quite 'the tune what I wrote'. Who cares? They made it famous and the words 'positive thinking' are now more identified with Morecambe & Wise than with Norman Vincent Peale.

Many years ago, we went to Biagi's Restaurant in Upper Berkeley Street, London. Eric, with two or three others, was halfway through his meal at a nearby table. By then, he and Ernie were regularly performing 'Positive Thinking'. Shortly after we re-ceived the menu, Eric crawled on all fours over to our table and shouted in my ear, 'HERE'S SOME POSI-TIVE THINKING – DON'T HAVE THE FISH!' He then crawled back again to his own table. Being a small restaurant no one could miss seeing or hearing him. Only Eric Morecambe could do that and not be asked to leave on account of disorderly conduct.

Jackie and I also had the pleasure of entertaining Ernie and his wife Doreen on our boat in Sydney when he toured Australia with his one-man show, following Eric's untimely death. (Actually, it was really a 'two-man' show because Ernie 'wisely' included many hilarious Eric and Ernie TV clips.)

PAUL ZENON

If you read one of their scripts never having seen Morecambe & Wise, it might well strike you as not being particularly funny. It's the bits that *aren't* said that make it – Eric's (apparent) deviation from script and his priceless reactions, body language, double-takes and pauses. His face seems to paint a vivid picture of his thought processes as they happen and builds huge anticipation for the next line; it's like the whirring of cogs before the clock chimes or an anticipatory drum roll before the cymbal crash – and you know it's going to be a big one by the expression of serene, amused confidence on Ernie's face that could only come from decades treading the boards in tandem.

Much comedy these days has a fairly narrow

demographic; different niches for different social groups. For younger people it tends to be intellectually clever; politically or socially astute, or generally confrontational or cruel in some way – there's usually a target. It's difficult to imagine a group of teenagers or younger kids these days being held spellbound as we were by a couple of middle-aged blokes just being plain daft; they had no agenda other than laughter. What Eric and Ernie did have above all else was warmth: behind Eric's bluster and mischief and Ernie's pomposity and pretension, there was never a hint of real animosity towards anyone – not even Des O'Connor!

CAROLE TODD

I worked on one edition of *The Morecambe & Wise Show* for Thames Television at their then Teddington Studios. It was a *Thoroughly Modern Millie* routine with Morecambe & Wise, Joanna Lumley and ten girl dancers.

Joanna was petrified because, although she was a beautiful actress, she really wasn't a dancer.

It was the usual type of big routine and featured Eric and Ernie taking Joanna, wearing her frilly dress, to buy her a new fur coat. Gareth Hunt, Joanna's co-star from *The New Avengers*, also made an appearance at the end of the routine.

Eric made me feel very comfortable, so encouraging. He really brought the best out of you, and made you feel like they wanted you to be there.

A photo of Eric, Ernie and I was given to me later. Eric had signed it: 'With love, Eric Morecambe'. It was very lovely, especially as, to my great regret, I never got to work with them again due to other work commitments.

RICHARD DIGANCE

L ike most British people of a certain age, I was brought up on Morecambe & Wise. They were there for as long as I can remember, as a school-kid making me laugh through boring Christmas Days after the Queen had successfully negotiated her auto-cue for another year. Strangely I didn't appreciate the value of Ernie Wise until I was in show business myself. He was 'the stooge', the straight man without whom Eric couldn't fire his bullets of hilarity and the man who held the timing together. I met Ernie when he was doing a gardening programme and treasured the opportunity to be in the presence of a comedy genius, half of the greatest duo the world has ever seen. They made me laugh more than Abbott and Costello and Laurel and Hardy, and as a young kid growing up in the East End I loved them as much as Geoff Hurst and Martin Peters.

Did I ever meet them both? Yes, but only on a few occasions and I only worked with them the once at a charity show, which I seem to remember being at a nightclub in Luton in the shadows of the M1. Jim Davidson told me that night I would never meet any others more professional or alluring to an audience, and he was absolutely right. It will always remain an honour.

LINDA WILLIS

From when I was eight years old, my dad worked at ATV Borehamwood. During this time I was privileged to be invited to watch the shows recorded there. My dad got the tickets, and my mum and I happily sat in the audience watching the very best of the best! TV was all about quality in those days.

One of the funniest programmes was, of course, *Two of a Kind: The Morecambe & Wise Show*!

I recall on one occasion sitting in the audience seating area at ATV, in what I think was Studio D. In those days, it was raised up but with gaps in the side for you to see through. My mum and I took our seats, smiling with expectation of what was to come, and we were not disappointed! For, from the minute Eric Morecambe and Ernie Wise appeared, we were in stitches. Laughing uncontrollably till the tears rolled down our cheeks! My dad was watching from behind the scenes.

After the first part of the show was recorded, I looked down from my lofty perch in the audience watching as Eric walked slowly from the set and carefully picked up and lit up a big pipe! He paced up and down, puffing away, and looking so worried and anxious, and I thought, 'Why are you so concerned? You were absolutely brilliant! You have nothing at all to worry about whatsoever! You are the funniest man on the planet!' All I wanted to do was clamber down from my seat, and fling my arms round him and give him a great big hug – and tell him that!

My dad adored Morecambe & Wise, especially Eric, because they were on the same wavelength! He would repeat jokes or sketches that Eric had thought up, and of course in those days Sid and Dick were also working on the scripts. But Eric was the superstar, although he never, ever acted that way. Anyone who met him or watched him work could see that he was a natural comic genius who could make you fall about just by standing still!

The BBC liked to think that they invented Morecambe & Wise, but it was Lew Grade of ATV who

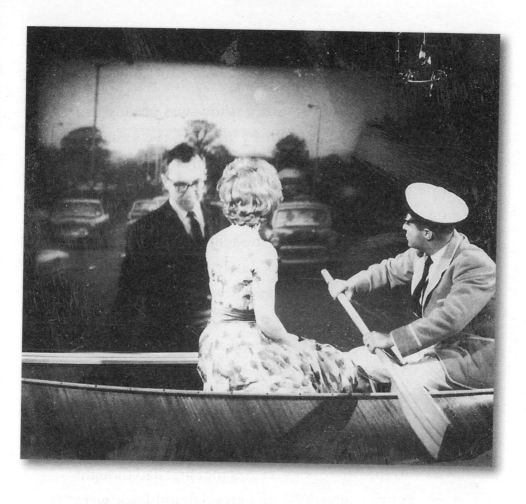

It's hard to place this photo, a still from an early TV show. – GM

set the ball rolling. I worked at ATV for seven years when I was older, and closely with Lord Grade. He was an exceptional entrepreneur who could spot talent a million miles away, and made stars of people like Tom Jones and Engelbert Humperdinck. I think perhaps in those days gone by the BBC were still into a strictly 'BBC accent' which, of course, Eric did not possess – not at all! But ATV and Lew could see the diamond behind the Northern accent, and he polished it till it sparkled!

I remember vividly the day that the BBC took Morecambe & Wise from ATV, because my dad returned from work deeply moved and very upset. My mum and I were so concerned – what could have possibly occurred to cause him such distress? Had someone died? Was someone ill? With a look of such sadness he replied: 'We've lost Morecambe & Wise – to the BBC.'

My former husband and I were decorating our hallway in Bushey Heath when the news came through on the radio that Eric Morecambe had died. It felt to me as though I had lost a member of my own family.

CARL GRESHAM

··

Definitely the biggest double act I ever worked with, they could draw a crowd and keep them enthralled. I remember talking to their agent Billy Marsh before I first used them. I requested a couple of photographs to use in my promotions. Billy asked why I wanted photographs – as surely the public knew what they looked like!

Eric told me about the car-park attendant at the BBC who had his favourites, which meant some would get a parking place and others might not. George was his name. He had lost an arm in the war. One day he shouted to Eric after he had parked his car if there was any chance of tickets for the Christmas show they were going to record. Eric shouted back, 'No.' George was shocked and asked why. Eric said, 'What's the point? You've only got one arm and you won't be able to clap!' Eric never missed a chance for a gag. If you were wondering, George did get his tickets.

Carl Gresham and Eric pose for a photo.

HANNAH GORDON

I had just made the first series of *My Wife Next Door*. My agent rang and said I had been asked to appear in *The Morecambe & Wise Show*, but I had to be there that afternoon. Another actress had said no, and no one had ever turned them down before. I was very nervous but Eric was smashing and very kind to me.

Eric was genuinely funny in real life – so funny and quick. Eric once said to me: 'I walk into a room and people expect me to be funny.'

Morecambe & Wise couldn't have done what they did without all their experience. They served a wonderful apprenticeship. They were such a team. I learned so much from them.

When I appeared on *Morecambe & Wise's Christmas Show* in 1980 for Thames Television, we

rehearsed at Richmond Football Ground. We had such a good time that I remember saying to Peter Barkworth, who was also on the show: 'Can you believe we're getting paid for this?!'

RICHARD STONE

···

Anglia Television had been keen to make a prime-time documentary of my artistic journey from postman's son to, apparently, a favourite Court artist. However, they were somewhat at a loss as to who would be a suitable subject for me to paint for the programme. An Anglia Television executive suggested that he would ask his friend Eric Morecambe if there was any possibility that he would subject himself to the scrutiny not only of the TV camera, but also of an almost unknown young artist.

After an initial meeting with me at his home in Harpenden, Hertfordshire, Eric agreed to give it a go, and a series of sittings were booked and a studio hired in a disused warehouse overlooking Tower Bridge. The filming of *Morecambe and Stone* was an

ABOVE *Eric's portrait, which still hangs in my mother's house. It was not, however, the first that he sat for. I currently have the first one locked away in storage.* – GM

BELOW *The portrait, the artist (Richard Stone) and the subject!* – GM

174

incredibly enjoyable experience. Eric's spontaneous joking and his reminiscences of his childhood days on stage and the insight into the influences shaping his comic genius were fascinating.

Eric was happy to participate in the film for no fee other than the portrait itself, if he liked it. However, there was to be one proviso. As the credits rolled over his portrait at the end of the film, he insisted on adding a 'd' to the end of my surname. This was a final comic touch that didn't remain on the picture for posterity.

TAMMY JONES

Born in North Wales, I began singing at a very early age. I went on to become a regular on both radio and television in my native Wales. Guest spots then followed on British television with stars including Benny Hill, Tom Jones, The Bachelors, Dick Emery and Morecambe & Wise.

I have lovely memories of Morecambe & Wise. For instance, the night before we were recording their show, I was singing away at a rehearsal and I could hear Eric and Ernie whispering and joking behind me, saying that they should have brought sandwiches as they would be there all night as I was singing a slow song! There I was trying to keep a straight face and trying to sing but just wanting to laugh!

*Eric and my mother Joan at a charity event with 'the voice'
himself, Tom Jones. Eric and Tom got on very well together,
once flying back from Portugal on the same flight. This
particular shot of them probably just pre-dates Tom's
highly memorable, oft-screened appearance on a Morecambe
& Wise show, when Eric and Ernie became his backing
singers! – GM*

178

MIKE YARWOOD

I started at ATV just after Morecambe & Wise left to go to the BBC, then I went to the BBC and then later to Thames – which Eric and Ernie switched to after their days at the BBC. So we sort of followed each other around!

When I first met Eric, it was at the BBC. I told him that I was doing an impression of him nowadays and Eric asked: 'Are you doing me now?'

I used to watch people like Eric on TV as much as possible, but, if I couldn't 'get them' straight away, then I wouldn't include them in my act.

I used to always impersonate Eric while wearing a top hat because Eric had less hair than me and I didn't want to wear a wig!

Incidentally, I memorably recall impersonating Eric as part of a three-week run at the Talk of the Town during the early 1970s.

In 1968, I appeared in the *Royal Variety Performance*. I was not down to do this show, but Eric had a heart attack, and I happened to be at the

Former Prime Minister and leader of the Conservative
Party, Edward Heath. Eric clearly wants him to join the Des
O'Connor fan club and push the membership up to two! – GM

London Palladium. Eric and Ernie were doing two spots in the show, and as stand-ins Frankie Howerd took one and I did the other. My greatest thrill was that I was in the No.1 dressing-room, because it's part of theatre ethics that if you replace a performer you naturally go into his room. I wasn't the senior star in the show, but I was in the star's dressing-room, sharing it with Engelbert Humperdinck and Des O'Connor and Frankie Howerd – no hardship there. It was a room I had visited before.

Although I don't perform my act professionally now, I still impersonate people like Eric at dinner parties. And I kept that black top hat I used to wear when I impersonated him. And, although I don't wear it, I keep it as a souvenir. I also still have the fez that I wore when impersonating Tommy Cooper.

Eric's wife never seemed to laugh at Eric's jokes. My wife didn't laugh at my act either. Wives of comedians never seem to laugh at their husbands!

L–R: *Sir Harry Secombe, Eric, Terry Wogan, Margaret Thatcher, David Evans and Anthony Swainson of the Lord's Taverners.*

PAMELA SALEM

eeting Eric Morecambe is my best memory of
the whole film *Night Train to Murder*. He was
a wonderful human being. I cannot praise him too
highly. He was even funnier off screen than on. He
was a naturally generous and kind-hearted person,
who had time for everyone, an enthusiasm for life,
and personally I feel privileged to have met him.

When I first interviewed for the part of Cousin
Zelda in the film, I reminded him that my husband,
Michael O'Hagan, had acted with him twenty years
previously in panto, and at that time, Eric, as a
surprise, had given dinner jackets to him and the
property master, so they could go to the black-tie
charity affair to which they had been invited. And
Eric had tucked money into their pockets so they

could buy drinks and hold their own at the Comedians' Table. Eric remembered Michael, and, when I told him he had driven me to the interview, he jumped up and insisted Michael came in. After all those years, he still had time for his 'mates'.

I used to try and spend as much time with Eric off stage as well as on because he was such an interesting and humorous man – he came at life from such a refreshing and insightful angle, and he made me laugh when we acted together.

Unfortunately, I did not think the script was funny, and I was really worried that our scenes would not work. When I voiced my concerns, I was told that this was light entertainment and Joe would get it together in the editing. I did not feel at all happy doing the film, although I was delighted to meet up with the truly gifted Kenneth Haigh again, and we had a really good cast. Lysette Anthony was one of the most beautiful girls you could hope to see, and even with such a good cast the film did not work. At the time I had not worked in light entertainment and so I thought it must be my inexperience that made me so anxious, but unfortunately my instincts were correct. Eric and Ernie shelved the film themselves and it only came out after Eric had died. I have not seen it – I do not want to depress myself!

Eric presented with a collection of photos by the Lord's Taverners.

Nothing is wasted and I learned a lot, including to trust my own instincts, and I had the joy of meeting and spending time with Eric Morecambe. I also got to keep a beautifully comfortable pair of high shoes that were made for me – those were the days! – so much so that I went to the shoe shop that had made my last, thanks to Thames Television, and I ordered another pair, which were a disaster. I have no idea why, extremely uncomfortable and I think I gave them away!! These days I would have taken them back and made them do it again, but I wasn't so brave then!

The cast and crew did socialise together in the bar at Thames Television in Teddington. It was always one of the favourite places to work as it was situated on a beautiful spot on the River Thames, and everyone treated you very well. I didn't know how we lunched in the bar in those days and then went to do an afternoon's work!! My method is much more disciplined these days but then I am a lot older and I hope wiser!

ROGER WASH

Eric started to watch Luton in the late 1960s in an attempt to indoctrinate son Gary to the game. The Luton secretary at the time made sure that Eric's seat was next to the directors' box, leading to him being asked to the Boardroom for drinks after each game. This, in turn, led to him becoming a director of the club.

With *The Morecambe & Wise Show* playing to huge audiences and the 'Hatters' doing well on the pitch, it was a marriage made in heaven. Eric mentioning his beloved football team at every opportunity was the best PR a club could wish for.

Although Eric took his director's role at the club very seriously, he obviously loved an audience and played up to the cameras at every opportunity. In

Eric and Joan at a Luton Town FC bash. It looks like Luton hero Ricky Hill that Eric is making it deliberately difficult for future archivists to confirm. – GM

those days, the club used to charter special trains to away games for the princely sum of 25/- (£1.25). And wherever we went the players and officials took up a couple of carriages as well. My abiding memory is of Eric walking up and down the corridors chatting to the supporters, practising his paper-bag trick, adjusting people's glasses and generally acting the fool for hours on end.

ROBIN KING

Eric, in his capacity as chairman of Luton Town, was a frequent visitor at the old Baseball Ground in Derby. My father, who was appointed as director in 1947 and became chairman on a number of occasions (it was a one-year rotating role), ended as life president. In the 1950s, he made a point of going to all away matches, and took me with him; it was during one of these visits that he first met Eric and they became life-long friends. Whenever Eric was in Derby (every Christmas he appeared in panto at Derby Hippodrome for a number of years), he always made a point of coming to Derby's home games and, after a swift phone call to Dad, he was always seated in the directors' box as a visiting Luton Town director.

Eric with a photo of his favourite singing star! – GM

Model behaviour: Eric and a model help publicise a new shirt sponsor. – GM

At a Derby v. Arsenal game just after one Christmas, Eric was sitting behind Brian Clough and, not knowing (or caring) about Brian's hatred of being touched, he tapped Brian on the shoulder, and then said: 'Not taking many prisoners, are they?' after a particular hard-tackling bit of play. He then turned to my sister and me and went through his routine of smoking the pipe upside down, glasses on upside down, and the coin in the paper-bag trick. All to cover up any embarrassment caused by Brian's reaction!

Eric was a great man, and a wonderful character.

Author's note: It should be stressed that Brian Clough DID love Eric!

DENNIS KIRKLAND

··

Eric Morecambe was a very nervy person like Tony Hancock and most of the greats.

Eric used to come and have a drink with us at lunch with his crew and, before they went back to their rehearsal or whatever, used to sit down with Benny (Hill). And Eric used to say the same thing every time. He used to say: 'It's all based on fear, Ben,' and Ben would say: 'Fingernails and aspirins!' And the pair of them used to sit there moaning about their lot: 'How's it going?' 'Oh I don't know,' and all that and take the mickey out of me, which was fine.

After a show, Eric would come up to the bar, and Ernie of course, and their various marvellous guest stars, and within seconds Eric would be wondering: 'Could we have done that bit better?' and 'Is there any chance of doing that again?' Or: 'We'll never do that again on the next show, I promise you.' So the euphoria with people like that lasted for minutes. A lot of them are like that. Eric Morecambe was one of the funniest men we ever presented to the world and people don't understand that there was tension behind it all – and nor should they. All they want is their hero on the telly.

VICKI MICHELLE

Eric and Ernie were quite simply two of the most brilliant comedy performers of all time and the perfect foils for each other, a team in every sense. To me they were the epitome of situation comedy – it didn't matter what situation you put them in, they would work their touch of genius and make it funny. I also used to marvel at the lengths they could get their guest stars to go to on their shows, particu larly Glenda Jackson and Shirley Bassey.

I often used to bump into them in the infamous BBC canteen or rehearsal rooms during my early days at the BBC. The first time I met Eric properly was at a charity event. He was so gentle and down to earth. In more recent years I have had contact with Joan Morecambe at fundraising events given

197

by such organisations as The Lady Taverners and Lady Ratlings. I am also fortunate to know Ernest Maxin through my connection with The Heritage Foundation. He was their producer at the Beeb from the mid-1970s and masterminded The Boys' tremendous success from behind the scenes.

As for my favourite sketch, where do you start? Actually, I loved the opening café scene from the film *The Intelligence Men*. Picture Eric trying to serve coffee, catch the gist of a major espionage plot, wrestle with the pronunciation of the Russian enemy spy department, memorise a theme from a well-known ballet and get Ernie to pay for his tea all at the same time! It still has me falling about. And who could forget the trademark slap Eric inflicted on Little Ern. I often wondered if it hurt, so I tried it on my husband. He confirmed it does!

Yes, they brought sunshine; yes, they brought laughter. In fact, they made you laugh out loud, not just smile or giggle, and they still do with their legacy today – but, more than that, they brought families together to share in it. Quite an epitaph.

MADELINE SMITH

Both Eric and I had worked with the director of *The Passionate Pilgrim*, Charles Wallace, before, in 1979, when Charles was making *Betjeman's Britain* ('an acclaimed musical dramatisation of poems by Sir John for Anglia Television'). The other guests on the programme were Peter Cook and Susannah York.

I was just about to start college full-time when filming began, and at the time I thought this film was to be my swan song from acting. I remember thinking what a wonderful swan song it was to be working with Eric Morecambe!

When we started filming *The Passionate Pilgrim* in October 1982, Eric was showing signs of fatigue. Fellow cast member Tom Baker used to keep him up

These photos come from Charles Wallace's film The Passionate Pilgrim, *narrated by John Le Mesurier and co-starring
Tom Baker and Madeline Smith. The original idea was to
make three films with the main protagonists in constant
battle at different points in time and location. Sadly, Eric
died shortly after completing the first.* – GM

so late talking and I was so worried about him. But when Eric had an audience he was unstoppable.

Eric had no airs at all. We spoke like old friends when we were filming at Hever Castle. He was a humble and modest man. Fame had not gone to his head at all and he was a sweetheart to me.

He adored doing the film and put his heart and soul into it. Eric loved to work and pushed himself very hard rehearsing 'prat falls' for the film.

For part of the filming at Hever Castle, it was chilly and damp, and for at least some of the shots I can remember the make-up lady standing with an umbrella over Eric and me!

Eric was VALIANT – a real *soldier*. He fought on, putting his life 'on the line' to bring everything he could to his part in *The Passionate Pilgrim*. Despite his health problems, he never ever complained, but was concerned for *my* wellbeing because we worked so hard.

I totally adored Eric and I can say that with my hand on my heart. He was so funny in real life – a genuinely funny man. What an inspiration to me he was.

TANIA GLYDE

The photo on the next page was taken in the very hot summer of 1976, or 'the drought' as it was known. I was ten years old and my parents had taken me to a Lord's Taverners' charity cricket match at, I think, Burghley House near Stamford in Lincolnshire.

You paid to have your picture taken with some of the famous people playing in the charity match. I had my photo taken with both Eric Morecambe and Tom Baker, who was then Dr Who. I asked Tom if he wore his long scarf to play cricket. He told me he left the famous garment in the pavilion as he was worried about tripping over it.

Eric gave me his pint to hold for the picture. I was shy, I think, and we never drank beer at home!

Eric with Tania Glyde at a Lord's Taverners' charity cricket match. She had been in the autograph queue and kindly sent me this photo for inclusion in the book.

Eric had played cricket at many charity matches down the years, but when joining the Taverners, he made the decision to stick to using his image to sell the charity rather than continue to join in the actual sporting event. I will always remember a Taverners' cricket match at Blenheim Palace in the mid-seventies, and the commentator's voice coming over the speakers: 'And Eric Morecambe is STILL signing autographs!' – GM

ERIC MORECAMBE

VALERIE VAN OST

··

think myself very fortunate to have worked with so many of the great comedians and comedy acts during my career: Spike Milligan, Arthur Haynes, David Jason, Jimmy Tarbuck, Charlie Drake, Harry Secombe, Cannon and Ball, Jerry Lewis, Sid Caesar, Frankie Howerd – the list goes on. They were all exceptional, all extremely professional and all artistes that will be remembered as amongst the great comics of the period. I am very proud to have known them all.

There are two names that hold very special memories for me: Eric Morecambe and Ernie Wise, two very 'ordinary' people with extraordinary talents. The warmth the public saw on their TV screen came from two of the most endearing and charming characters off stage. But the brilliant timing and seeming ease with which they worked, and which earned them their extraordinary popularity, was hard won.

I worked with The Boys in three of their TV shows for ATV. These hilariously funny shows were directed by Colin Clews and written by Sid and Dick.

Although the shows were recorded before a live audience in the studio, there were always several runs in the studio for the benefit of the lighting and camera crews. Every time a sketch was run through, The Boys managed in some way to make it seem fresh and different. Each felt as if it was a 'first run', with that little added something that would have the crews falling about laughing. I had never seen such a spontaneous reaction to any comic I had worked with before. It was quite exceptional and made rehearsals great fun. I imagine that it was also a very useful gag-tester for Eric and Ernie.

In putting together my memories for this book, I realised how much of my career in the business I had forgotten. But Morecambe & Wise I will never forget, not just because of their professionalism and comedy skills, but for their kindness and consideration. Support artistes and crews alike thought the world of them.

Harry Secombe, Terry Wogan and Eric at a Lord's Taverners charity event.

NICKI EDWARDS

....

My meeting with Eric Morecambe was, to say the least, unplanned. The whole family were huge Morecambe & Wise fans – it was a show we all watched together – but my mother totally idolised Eric and cried for days when he died. She truly felt his like would never be seen again.

One summer, when I was about thirteen, Eric came to open the annual fête at one of the local nursing homes. It was an event my mother was determined to go to, as she thought it would be her only chance to see the great man in the flesh. My father, a psychiatric nurse on shift work, was unable to come with us but did drive us over to the home and drop us off in the car park.

While we were getting our bearings in the car

park, another car drew in at snail's pace, flanked by a few people running alongside. It came to a halt and Eric got out. Someone shouted, 'It's him!' and, almost immediately, dozens of people came from nowhere and completely engulfed him. A couple of helpers pushed their way in but did nothing to ease the situation, and Eric, my mother and I ended up pinned up against the car.

Now, my mother – Betty Smith – was not a large lady in those days, but she did have a formidable presence (think Peggy Mount). She drew herself up to her full 5 ft and bellowed something along the lines of: 'This is ridiculous, the poor man can't move. He needs to be sat at a table, preferably in a room with an outside window where people can form an orderly queue for their autographs.'

Lo and behold, we were ushered away to said room and that's exactly what happened. The upshot was, my mother and I found ourselves in the same room drinking tea with him as he chatted to all concerned. I still have the autograph he gave me to this day. On reflection, I do wonder if those in charge actually thought we were members of his party, but Eric certainly didn't give us away!

JAN CLENNELL

....

As a dancer on an edition of Morecambe & Wise's Thames Television shows, my memory of the rehearsal period is that it was fun and light-hearted but very professional when we were practising the dance numbers.

Both Eric Morecambe and Ernie Wise respected us dancers; they sat with us and we all ate lunch together and I felt included in their chats. That was very special.

Both Morecambe and Wise seemed very close and happy throughout the period of the show. It was a very enjoyable time for me personally, especially as they were my dad's favourite act.

ERIC MORECAMBE'S NOTEBOOKS II

The Sullivan Vent routine!

This relates to Eric and Ernie's 1960s visits across the pond to NYC to appear as British guest stars on the Ed Sullivan show off Broadway. Eric and Ernie already had a vent act, so this development, which he has marked as 'DONE, vg' (very good) is really interesting to me. I don't know if a recording exists and very little of their Sullivan work appears to from what I am told when enquiring into their 1964–68 annual visits to the States.

~~JODRELL BANK FOR NOTHING~~

KRL 'HE'S THE FELLA WITH THE BIG EARS ISN'T HE?

KRN. HE'S THE WHAT?

KRL GORDON.

KRN HE'S THE FELLA WITH THE BIG EARS?

KRL OH YOU'VE NOTICED THEM AS WELL!

KRN. THAT NOT A NICE THING TO SAY!

KRL WELL HIS EARS ARE BIG - AS A MATTER OF FACT THEY'RE SO BIG YOU COULD DRINK OUT OF THEM. HE LOOKS LIKE A TAXI WITH THE DOORS OPEN. NO WONDER THEY CALL HIM JODRELL BANK.

KRN — NOW <u>THATS ENOUGH.</u>

SOMEONE SINGS THE LAST NOTE IN A GROUP AND ITS A VERY HIGH NOTE HE RISES BY A WIRE ABOUT 2'6" (SLOWLY) IN THE AIR

....

Ladies and gentlemen. Before I make this speech, you're looking at a very happy man (waving telegram). Because today, we had a happy event at home. Yes, my wife has just got a job. I'm thrilled.

You can never tell when a catastrophe will strike. I remember a friend of mine in this very building only last week was stood just over there ... Just stood there, and the very next day he was married.

They say clever men make the best husbands – that to me is ridiculous. Clever men don't become husbands.

At 20 years, women are like Africa, hot and tempestuous. At 45 they are like Europe, crumbling but still interesting. At 70, women are like (local place). Everybody knows where it is, but nobody wants to go there anymore.

The slowest person on earth is a nudist climbing through a barbed-wire fence.

214

SPEECH.

LADIES & GENTLEMEN. BEFORE I MAKE THIS
SPEECH. YOUR LOOKING AT A VERY HAPPY (LEAVING THE)
MAN. BECAUSE TODAY: WE HAD A VERY
HAPPY EVENT AT HOME: — YES MY WIFE
HAS JUST GOT A JOB. I'M THRILLED:

YOU CAN NEVER TELL WHEN A CATASTROPHE WILL
STRIKE. I REMEMBER. A FRIEND OF MINE IN
THIS VERY BUILDING ONLY LAST WEEK WAS
STOOD JUST OVER THERE. JUST STOOD THERE
AND THE VERY NEXT DAY HE WAS MARRIED.

THEY SAY CLEVER MEN MAKE THE BEST
HUSBANDS — THAT TO ME IS RIDICULOUS
CLEVER MEN DON'T GET MARRIED. BECOME
HUSBANDS.
AT 20 YRS. WOMEN ARE LIKE AFRICA.
HOT AND TEMPESTUOUS, AT 45 THEY ARE
LIKE EUROPE CRUMBLING BUT STILL
INTERESTING — AT 70 WOMEN ARE LIKE
(LOCAL PLACE). EVERYBODY KNOWS WHERE
IT IS, BUT NOBODY WANTS TO GO THERE
ANY MORE.
THE SLOWEST PERSON ON EARTH IS A NUDIST
CLIMBING THRO A BARBED-WIRE
FENCE.

215

....

Ideas for Xmas Show 1974

Author's note: The Frank Sinatra idea was used in a BBC show. 'Peter and The Wolf', with André Previn, was not.

It's interesting to note that the heading on this page of Eric's notes is 'IDEAS FOR XMAS SHOW '74.' There WAS no Christmas show 1974 – Eric had flu, and they had to cancel it just before it was due to be recorded. The annual treat was replaced by a Morecambe & Wise clip-driven show hosted by presenter Michael Parkinson.

Ideas for Xmas show 74?

SONG WITH PRETTY AND FAMOUS GIRL.
'ONLY MAKE BELIEVE' VRY HOLLYWOD
WHITE DRESS
(WORDS) DICKY Q ×××××?

HIM. ONLY MAKE BELIEVE THAT I LOVE
YOU

GIRL ONLY MAKE BELIEVE THAT YOU LOVE
ME

HIM. COULDN'T I.

GIRL WOULDN'T YOU?

WHILE. HADN'T HE?[1] DIDN'T HE?[3]
SONG.
"IF I HAD A TALKING PICTURE OF YOU"
FRAME.

SOUND OF MUSIC LOCATION
SONG WHEN JULIE ANDREWS COMES OVER
BROW OF THE HILL'. WHILE OR J.A. AND
LINDA AS ONE OF THE KIDS!
OR FAMOUS STAR AS J.A. AND LINDA & ONE OF THE KIDS
WHEN CAMERA PULLS OUT'. IT'S REALLY A RUBBISH
DUMP. OR A STRAIGHT LINE IN HUMBLE TOWN.
THE HILLS ARE ALIVE TO THE SOUND OF MUSIC'

217

....

They say, cast the bread upon the water and it comes back a hundred fold. I did that. I threw a loaf of bread on the water, and it worked. But what do you do with a hundred wet loaves?

Anyone who sleeps like a baby never had one.

Two weeks ago I saw my wife kissing the butcher. Last week it was the grocer. This morning it was the postman. But I'm not worried – my turn will come! But why she kisses the butcher, the grocer and the postman I'll never know. It's the rent man we owe money to!

This tie happens to be 110 years old. I know it's 110 years old – my wife made it.

Nowadays I don't smoke cig. I drink very little. I don't gamble or swear. And I make all my own dresses.

218

THEY SAY CAST THE BREAD UPON THE WATER AND IT COMES BACK A HUNDRED FOLD. I DID THAT. I THREW A LOAF OF BREAD ON THE WATER. AND IT WORKED. BUT WHAT DO YOU DO WITH A 100 WET LOAVES

ANYBODY WHO SLEEPS LIKE A BABY NEVER HAD ONE.
TWO WEEKS AGO I SAW MY WIFE KISSING THE BUTCHER. LAST WEEK IT WAS THE GROCER. THIS MORNING IT WAS THE POSTMAN. BUT I'M NOT WORRIED MY TURN WILL COME. BUT WHY SHE KISSES THE BUTCHER THE GROCER AND THE POSTMAN ~~FOR~~ ILL NEVER KNOW — TIL THE RENTMAN WE OWE MONEY TO.

THIS TIE HAPPENS TO BE 110 YEARS OLD. I KNOW ITS 110 YEARS OLD — MY WIFE MADE IT.

NOWADAYS I DONT SMOKE CIG. I DRINK VERY LITTLE. I DONT GAMBLE OR SWEAR. AND I MAKE ALL MY OWN DRESSES

· ·

Author's note: The piano gag became a much more simple idea when it was finally used as a bit in one of their shows. It becomes a solo pianist playing incredibly quickly. The gag is a sight gag. The number finishes and the soloist (Eric) reveals he has about twenty fingers on each hand.

23

PIANO - ERIC PLAYING PIANO. THE PIANO
HAS A GLASS FRONT - OR IT SEEMS LIKE
A GLASS FRONT BUT ITS A PROP PIANO
WHAT LOOKS LIKE THE REFLECTION IS ANOTHER
MAN AND WHEN ERIC FINISHES THE ROWS
IN THE PIANO WHEN HAVING BEEN PLAYING
AS A REFLECTION COME OUT AND PLAY
THE LAST TWO CHORDS WHILE ERIC'S
BEING DRAGGED AWAY FROM THE PIANO

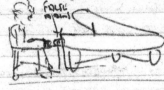

HANS WIGS

1   ERIC ANOTHER NEW ONE. I'M NOT KIDDING YOU
    HOW MANY'S THAT - 5 - 6 . HE'S GOT THEM ALL
    HANGING ON THE COAT HOCKS IN THE DRESSING
    ROOM ITS LIKE THE OUTSIDE OF A SUCCESSFUL
    RED INDIANS' TEPEE -

2   THAT 7 WIGS THAT I KNOW OF, HE'S
    GOT THEM ALL ON A TABLE IN THE DRESSING
    ROOM. WHEN HE PUTS HIS WHITE DRESSING
    GOWN ON ITS LIKE BEING WITH
    SNOW WHITE AND THE 7 DWARFS.

I'M PLAYING ALL THE

ERNIE: MY MOTHER HAS A WHISTLER. **ERIC:** NOW THERE'S A NOVELTY.

RIGHT NOTES... BUT

ERIC: HAD A BATH? **ERNIE:** YES. **ERIC:** NOT SEPTEMBER ALREADY, IS IT?

NOT NECESSARILY IN

ERIC: WHO'S YOUR TAILOR? **ERNIE:** WHY? **ERIC:** THAT WAS GOING TO BE MY SECOND QUESTION.

THE RIGHT ORDER!

YOU CAN'T SEE THE JOIN!

I bet you were glad to get here. **You're telling me!** I stood outside the station and took a deep breath of that fresh seaside air. **Marvellous!** One lung said to the other, 'That's the stuff I've been telling you about!' **Great!** Then I went directly to the beach, stripped off and ran straight into the sea. **Did it come up to your expectations? Just past them, actually –** that's the trouble with being so short. Then, would you believe it, a crab bit my toe! **Which one? I don't know – all crabs look alike to me.** I could hardly walk, so I decided to take a donkey ride. The bloke said, 'Don't take the one on the end – the rest'll fall over.' I said to him, 'Can I hire this donkey?' He said, 'Yes, there's a screw under the saddle.' So the donkey took you home? **No, just as far as the bus stop.** I got on the bus and I said to the driver, 'Do you stop at the Ritz Hotel?' And he said, 'What, on my wages?' **Did you ask him again? Yes, I said, 'Look, does this bus** stop at the harbour?' He said, 'If it doesn't, there's going to be one hell of a splash!' Didn't you explain to him that the Ritz Hotel is right next door to the harbour? **I did. And I invited him to drop in any time he liked. Preferably when the tide was out.** And when the lifeguard's looking in the opposite direction! **Did you know I used to be a lifeguard? Really? When? Last summer.** What did you do? **I saved women.** What for? **The winter.** Didn't you help any men? **Yes, I gave them the occasional woman. One day I had to rescue a drunken mermaid.** A drunken mermaid? **Yes, she'd had so much whisky on the rocks, she'd fallen into the sea.** How drunk was she? **She was absolutely legless.** I pulled her onto the beach and gave her artificial recreation. **Recreation is when you have fun. I'm no fool.** She had a fabulous figure, too. Really? **Yes, thirty-six, twenty-three, eighty-five pence a pound.**

HE'S NOT GOING TO SELL MUCH ICE-CREAM GOING AT THAT SPEED!

WHAT DO YOU THINK OF THE SHOW SO FAR?

RUGGISH!

I MADE ERN OUT OF A KIT AND RAN OUT OF WOOD WHEN I GOT TO THE LEGS

ERIC: I'VE JUST BOUGHT DES O'CONNOR'S NEW ALBUM. **ERNIE:** WHERE FROM? **ERIC:** BOOTS THE CHEMIST. **ERNIE:** DID YOU NEED A PRESCRIPTION? **ERIC:** I HAD TO GO TO THE POISON COUNTER.

ERNIE: DES O'CONNOR IS A SELF-MADE MAN. **ERIC:** I THINK IT'S VERY NICE OF HIM TO TAKE THE BLAME!

ERIC: THEY CALL HIM DES. IT'S SHORT FOR DESPERATE.

ERIC: DO YOU REMEMBER OUR FIRST MEETING? **ERNIE:** I DO. WE DECIDED TO TEAM UP AND HAVE A GO AT COMEDY. **ERIC:** WE SHOULD HAVE DONE THAT.

ERNIE: BUT YOU TOLD ME THE OTHER DAY SHE HAD A MILLION-DOLLAR FIGURE! **ERIC:** SHE HAS. TROUBLE IS, IT'S ALL IN LOOSE CHANGE.

ERIC: SHE'S A LOVELY GIRL, THOUGH. I'D LIKE TO MARRY HER, BUT HER FAMILY OBJECTS. **ERNIE:** HER FAMILY? **ERIC:** YES, HER HUSBAND AND FOUR KIDS.

NOT NOW, ARTHUR!

ERNIE: WHAT ARE YOU READING?

ERIC: MARK TWAIN.

ERNIE: WHO'S IT BY?

ERIC: HUCKLEBERRY FINN.

THIS BOY'S A FOOL!

ACKNOWLEDGEMENTS

My researcher, Paul Burton, and I would like to take this opportunity to sincerely thank the many individuals, companies, managements and agencies, etc. who have given us their time and help during the process of compiling this publication. It would be impossible to name them all. However, we would like to take a moment to credit just some of those who have made this book possible.

Firstly, we'd like to thank the estate of Eric Morecambe for their invaluable support.

Special thanks to my sister, Gail Morecambe, and comedienne and actress Miranda Hart for writing the foreword.

We're especially indebted to James Gillson and all at the Lord's Taverners, for their huge generosity in allowing us to use a number of photos from their archives, which relate to Eric's work for the charity.

Huge appreciation goes to Gareth Owen (Go-Photo) and Roger Wash (Club Historian, Luton Town FC), for granting us permission to use several photos relating to Eric's time as a director at the football club.

An extra-special thank you is due to Stan and Roger Stennett for providing us with material from their photographic archive.

Sincere thanks to producer/director Charles Wallace of Moving Image Company for allowing us to use stills from his film *The Passionate Pilgrim*.

We'd like to thank those individuals who have contributed their memories – and, in certain cases, photos – to this book. In alphabetical order: David Benson, Lionel Blair, Ted Childs, Jan Clennell, Brian Conley, Gemma Craven, Jim Davidson, Richard Digance, Ken Dodd, Nicki Edwards, Sir Bruce Forsyth, Tania Glyde, Hannah Gordon, Michael Grade, Carl Gresham, Tony Hatch, Eddie Izzard, Tammy Jones, Robin King, Dennis Kirkland, Burt Kwouk, Vicki Michelle, Ben Miller, Mavis Nicholson, Simon Pegg, Pamela Salem, Madeline Smith, Richard Stone, Jimmy Tarbuck, Carole Todd, Valerie Van Ost,

Roger Wash, Linda Willis, Victoria Wood, Mike Yarwood and Paul Zenon.

Our warmest thanks also go to the following. In alphabetical order: Jane Foster of the stills department at FremantleMedia, for giving us so much of her time, enthusiasm and patience; Ian Freeman; Jo Kirkland and the Dennis Kirkland Estate; Madame Tussauds, Blackpool; Seb Thompson at Brazen PR and TV-am/AP Archive.

And to anyone we might have overlooked, we give our eternal thanks.

Gary Morecambe

ABOUT THE AUTHORS

GARY MORECAMBE

Gary Morecambe is the son of comedian Eric Morecambe. He was born in London in 1956. After several years as a publicist for a leading theatrical agency, he became a full-time writer in 1982 and has published over twenty titles ranging from biography to fiction. In 2002, he was consultant to Kenneth Branagh's West End and Broadway hit *The Play What I Wrote.*

He has recently begun to direct short films based on his own published stories, and much of the rest of his time is spent working on Morecambe & Wise-related projects, from which he continues to derive the greatest pleasure. He has four grown-up children and lives with his partner, Margo, in Bath.

PAUL BURTON

A life-long fan of Eric Morecambe and Morecambe & Wise, Paul Burton was proud to be engaged to work as archivist, researcher and interviewer on *Eric Morecambe: Lost and Found*.

He has a prolific number of writing, producing and directing credits to his name. Since 1989, Paul has founded and run several of his own arts projects, including theatre, film and television projects. He now works as a freelance writer, consultant, filmmaker and film and TV historian.

His credits also include being engaged by the management of Elstree Studios to work on projects relating to the history of the complex; and co-writing a biography of the *Carry On* film actor Kenneth Connor.

Paul also wrote *The Morecambe & Wise Quiz Book*.

PICTURE CREDITS

··